This workbook was created and copyrighted in 2018 by Luther M. Maddy, It has been edited by Tammy Gammon, Ph.D.

Microsoft®, Access®, Word®, Excel®, Outlook®, and PowerPoint® are registered trademarks of Microsoft Corporation.

Conventions used:

Keyboard:
Keys to be pressed are enclosed in parenthesis such as: press (Enter).

Text to be typed, when included in an exercise step will be shaded. For example:
Type *No Fault Travel* and then press (Enter).

Mouse Operations:

Click: refers to clicking the left mouse button

Right-click: refers to clicking the right mouse button

Drag: refers to holding the left mouse button down and moving the mouse

Be sure to visit out our website: www.Pro-aut.com to order these workbooks in quantity.

Published by:

Pro-Aut Training and Consulting, Inc.
1024 Hemlock Ave.
Lewiston, ID 83501

You can also visit: www.LutherMaddy.com to contact the author, or see other resources available for this workbook.

Table of Contents

Lesson #1: A review of the basics

In this lesson you will review:

Creating Tables
Setting Field Properties
Creating Forms
Entering and Editing Data
Creating Queries
Creating Reports (mailing labels)

Lesson #1: A Review of the Basics

1. Start Microsoft Access and create a new, blank database named *No Fault Travel.*

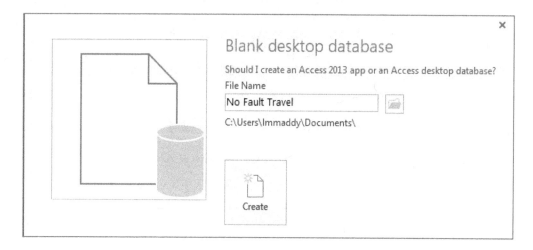

As you did in the *Access: The Basics* course, you will be creating a database from scratch rather than using a premade database template

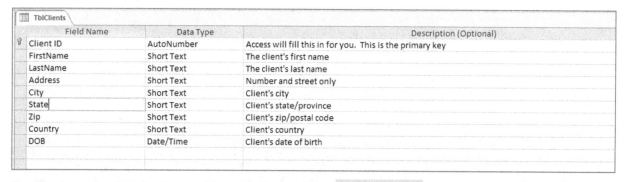

2. Enter design view. Name the table *TblClients* and create the field names, data types, and descriptions as shown.

In this course you will learn more about naming conventions. You may notice that the first three letters of the table name are *Tbl*. This will help you identify this object as a table later. For instance, there are times when you will see a list of all tables and queries in your database. If you have several tables and queries in your database, using the first three letters to identify the object type may help you quickly recognize which object you want to use.

3. **In design view and change the properties of the State field as shown below.**

General	Lookup	
Field Size	2
Format	>
Input Mask	
Caption	
Default Value	'ID'
Validation Rule	
Validation Text	
Required	No
Allow Zero Length	Yes
Indexed	No
Unicode Compression	Yes
IME Mode	No Control
IME Sentence Mode	None
Text Align	General

4. **Now change the field properties for each field to the values listed in the table below.**

Field	Size	Format	Default Value
FirstName	15		
LastName	25		
Address	30		
City	30		
State	2	> (greater than symbol)	ID
Zip	10		
Country	30		United States
DOB		Short Date	

In this course, we use the United States as the default value for country. If you are not in the US, just use this example as a guide for your own address structure. The *greater than* (>) symbol in the *Format* field property instructs Access to format the state in upper case letters, regardless of how it was entered.

5. **Save and close the clients table and create another table in design view named *TblAgents* with the fields as shown.**

Field Name	Data Type	Description (Optio
🔑 AgentID	AutoNumber	Access will fill this in. This is the primary key
FName	Short Text	Agent's first name
LName	Short Text	Agent's last name
CommissionRate	Number	Agent's trip commission rate

Notice you have abbreviated the field names for the agents' first and last names. Because you also have first and last names in the clients table, naming the fields differently will help you identify which table the data is coming from. If you were to create a query based on both tables, using different field names will help you identify which table that the first and last names come from.

6.   **Set the field properties of the *Commission Rate* field as shown:**

Field Properties

General   Lookup

Field Size	Double
Format	Percent
Decimal Places	Auto
Input Mask	
Caption	
Default Value	0
Validation Rule	
Validation Text	
Required	No
Indexed	No
Text Align	General

7.   **Close *TblAgents* and create another table named *TblTrips* as shown.**

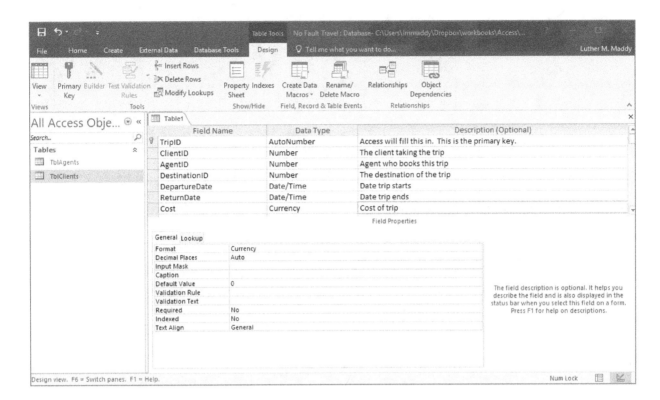

The *DestinationID* field will tie to a table you will create in a later lesson.

8.   Format both date fields as Short Date. Save and close this table.

You will now create a form for entering, viewing, and editing client records. You can use the Form Wizard as a starting form, if you use the *Columnar* layout. View the form in Design View and move and resize the fields. You should recall that you can move an individual control (label or text box) by clicking and dragging the square in the control's top left corner.

9.   Create a form, similar to the one below, which contains the fields in *TblClients*. Name the form *FrmClients*.

Like the tables you previously created, the first three letters *F-r-m* will later help you identify this Access object as a form in a list with other Access objects (i.e., tables, queries, reports, etc.).

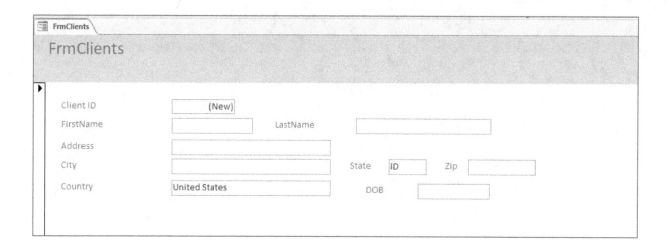

10. Use the *FrmClients* form to enter the following records.

John Smith
123 Main St.
Boise, ID 83705
4/12/1970

Susan Greene
443 Wilmont
Boise, ID 83706
11/30/1949

Calvin Brown
55 Walnut
Boise, ID 83705
12/28/1960

Carrie White
333 Poppy Dr.
Nampa, ID 83651
5/22/1988

Alvin Black
78 Maple
Boise, ID 83706
5/21/1958

Janice Johnson
8756 Overland
Nampa, ID 83651
5/22/1980

11. **Create a new query based on *TblClients* and name the query *QryAARPClients*. This query should display the names and addresses of all clients born before 1969.**

When creating this query you will need to enter the criteria as shown to only choose those clients born before 1969.

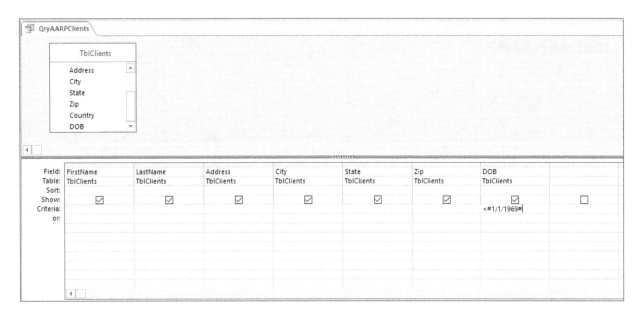

When you view the results of this query, you should see three clients, Susan, Calvin, and Alvin.

12. **Use the Labels tool in the Report group on the Create tab to create mailing labels using Avery 5160 as the label type. Base on the query *QryAARPClients*. Use the default name for these labels.**

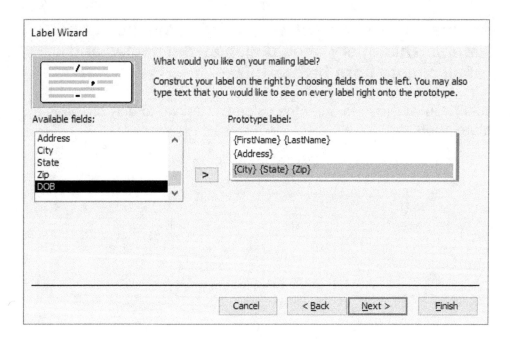

The result should resemble the image below. You did not include a comma (,) between the city and state to begin compliance with the United States Postal Service bulk mail rules.

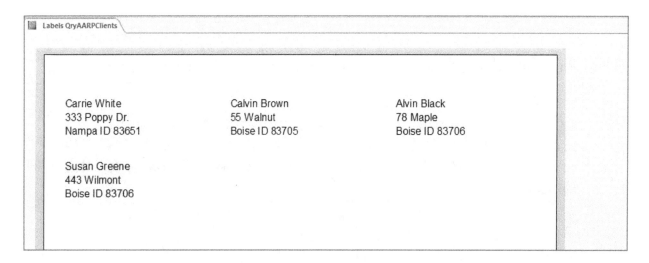

In this lesson, we reviewed several features discussed in *Access: The Basics*. You will use the database we created in the remaining lessons of this workbook.

Lesson #2: Lookup Fields and Validation Rules

In this lesson you will learn to:

Create Lookup Fields
Add Table Validation Rules

Lesson #2: Lookup Fields and Validation Rules

A lookup field creates a dropdown list, which makes entering and editing data much easier. Instead of the user entering data, the data is selected from a list of choices. Lookup fields also help ensure data integrity since the user chooses an allowed value from the dropdown list.

You can create lookup fields on forms or tables. One advantage of lookup fields in tables is that when you create forms based on the table, the lookup fields will automatically be included on the form. In addition, if you enter or edit data on the table directly using the Datasheet View, the lookup fields in the table will make entering data there easier.

The values for the dropdown list can be manually entered when the lookup field is created or the data can be obtained from another table. Using a table is the best choice because if you need to edit or add additional items to the dropdown list, editing existing values on or adding new records to a table is easy. If the values were entered directly into the list control, changes would have to be made to the programming code of the dropdown list. This adds a level of complexity and an additional skill you would have to learn.

In this lesson, you will create a new table that contains the trip destinations which can be booked through this travel agency. This table will provide the values for a dropdown list which is used when new trips are scheduled for clients.

1.   **Open the No Fault Travel database, if it is not already open. Create another table named *TblDestinations*.**

Although your goal is to create a dropdown list of the destinations, two fields will be included in the new table, *DestinationID* and *Destination*. *DestinationID* provides a unique identification number for each destination; it is the primary key with an AutoNumber data type.

2.   Enter the records as shown.

3.   Open *TblTrips* in Design View.

Creating a lookup field

Access makes it very easy to create a lookup field using the Lookup Wizard. In the next steps, you will link the *DestinationID* field in the *TblTrips* table to the destinations you entered into the *TblDestinations* table.

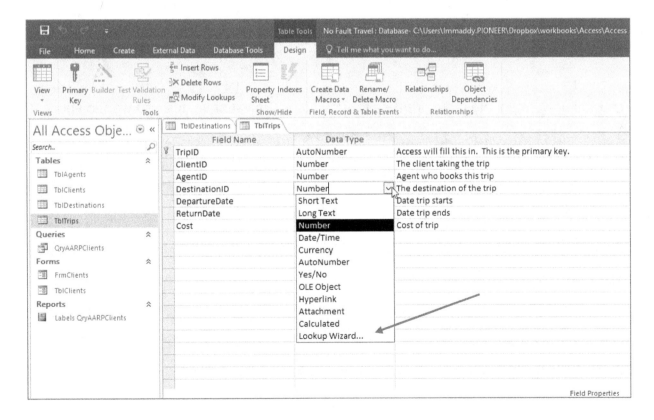

4.   **Click the drop down list button in the data type column of the DestinationID field. Then, select Lookup Wizard from the list of choices.**

Access will open the Lookup Wizard. The Lookup Wizard will guide you through the creation of a lookup field.

5.   **In the first step of the Lookup Wizard, be sure that the first option, "I want to look up values in a table or query", is selected and click Next.**

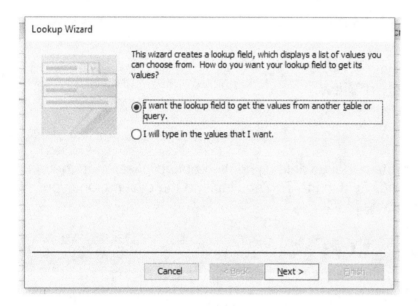

You will now select the table or query that contains the list of values you want displayed when you click the dropdown arrow for this field.

6.   **In this step of the Lookup Wizard, choose *TblDestinations* and click Next.**

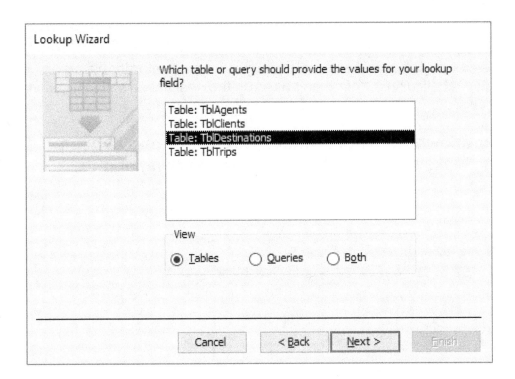

Next, you will select which fields from the table to display in the dropdown list. In this case, you will select both fields, *DestinationID* and *Destination*. The *DestinationID* will actually be stored in the field, but you will see the destination (not the ID) in the dropdown list.

7.   Select both fields with the double arrow that points right and then click Next.

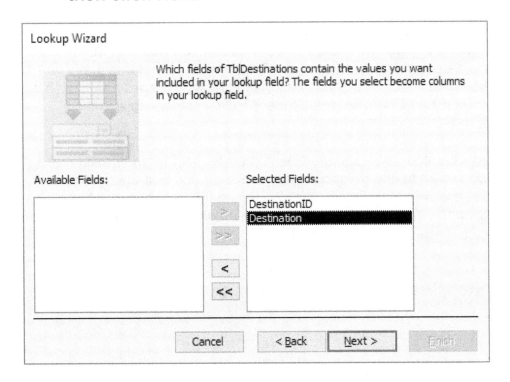

The next step in the wizard asks how you would like the records sorted for the dropdown list you are creating. You will sort the records in ascending order based on the destination field (alphabetically), rather than based on the destination's identification number field (numerically).

8.   Click the dropdown list arrow next to sort level 1 and choose *Destination*. Make sure the sort order is *Ascending* and then click Next.

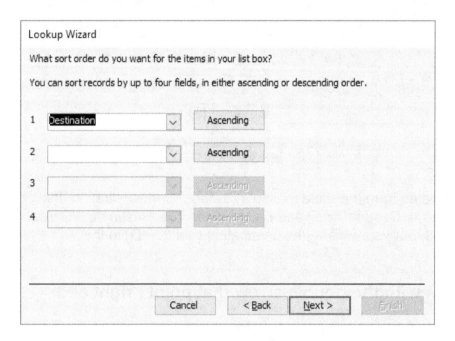

In the lookup field you are creating, Access will store the ID number for each destination. You will set up the lookup field so that the destination rather than its ID number appears in the dropdown list. Linking to an ID number field ensures that if you change the spelling of a destination in the *TblDestinations* table, the spelling will also be updated in the dropdown list and in all records of the *TblTtrips* table where that destination ID was stored.

Instead, you could have created *TblDestinations* with a single field for the destinations, which would have also served as the primary key. However, if you edit the destinations in the single-field table, the dropdown list should also reflect the changes, but the corresponding records in the *TblTrips* table will retain the original stored values and will not be updated because there is no unique identification number to serve as a cross-reference.

9.   In the next step, leave the *Hide key column* option selected. Click Next.

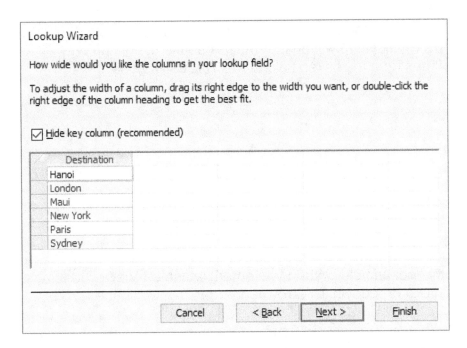

In the final step, the Lookup Wizard asks what to call this field. You have already named this field, so you keep the default name, *DestinationID*.

10.   When asked what to label the lookup field, make no changes and click Next.

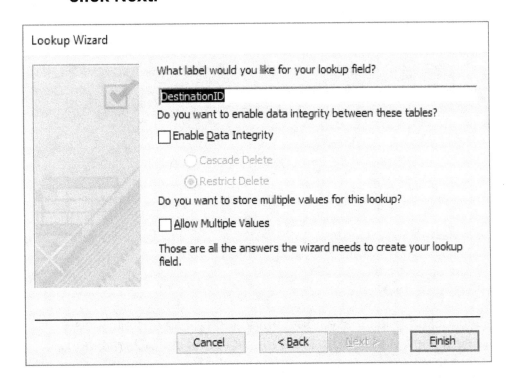

11.   When asked if you want to save the table, choose Yes.

You may notice that this dialog box informs you that Access will create a relationship between the two tables. This relationship will ensure that database users can only choose a destination in *TblTrips* from the linked field in the *TblDestinations*.

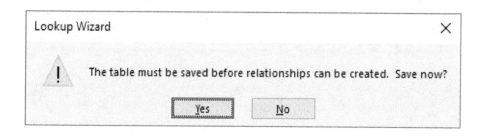

You are now ready to test the lookup field. When you enter Datasheet View, you should notice the destination field has a dropdown list arrow.

12.   Display the *Tbltrips* table in Datasheet View and verify that the *DestinationID* field is now a lookup field.

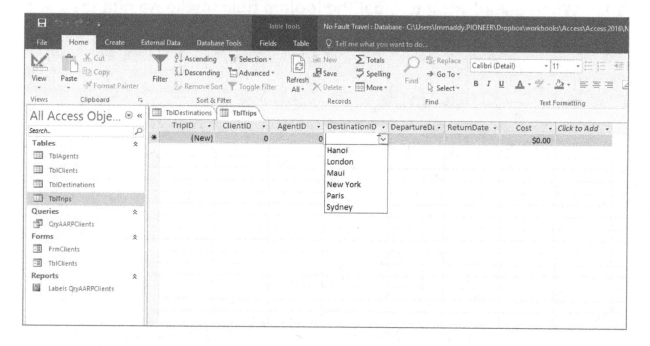

As you can see, creating lookup fields makes data entry and editing easier. It also ensures that only data contained in the linked table (destinations in *TblDestinations* here), can be entered into that field.

Two other fields in this table should also be lookup fields. These are the *ClientID* and the *AgentID* fields. In the next few steps, you will turn these fields into lookup fields and link them to the clients and agents tables using the Lookup Wizard.

13. Return to the Design View of *TblTrips*.

14. In the Data Type column of the *ClientID* field, click the dropdown list arrow and choose *Lookup Wizard*.

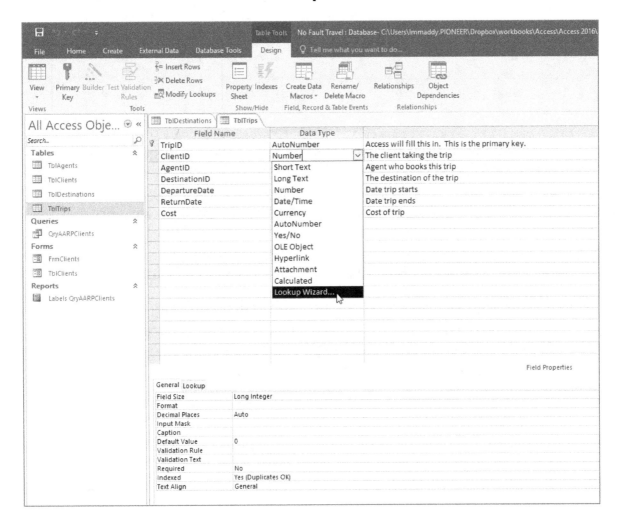

15. When the Lookup Wizard opens, select the option which links to a table or query. Click Next.

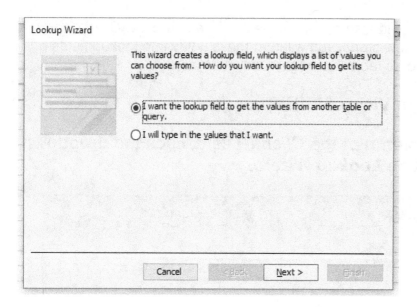

16. In the next step, choose the *TblClients* table and click Next.

Here you will select the fields to display in the dropdown list for the *ClientID* field. You will have Access store the client's identification number but display the client's first and last names for easier recognition.

17. Select the *ClientID*, *FirstName*, and *LastName* fields.

You can select an individual field by selecting it in the left column and then clicking the single arrow pointing to the right. You can also double click a field to select it.

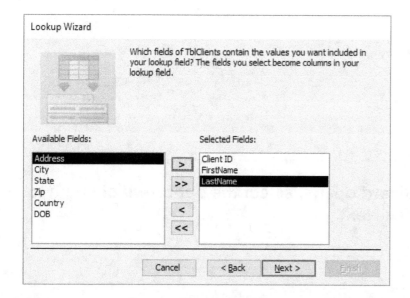

18. Sort the records by LastName and click Next.

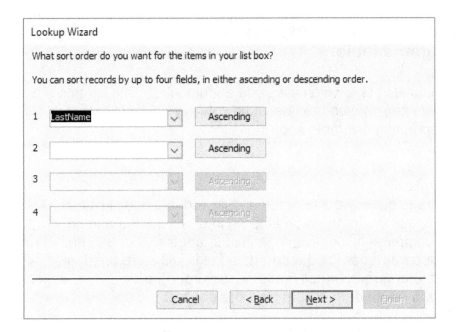

19. **Leave the *Hide* key column option selected and click Next.**

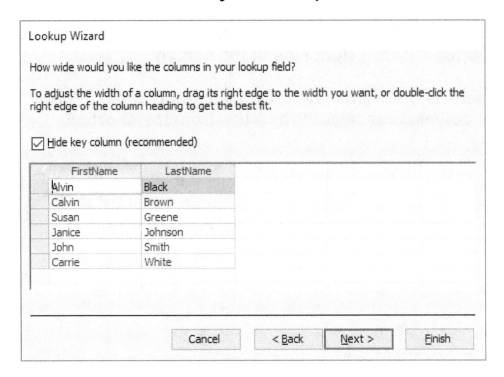

20. **Choose the default name for this field and click Finish. Answer "Yes" when Access asks if you want to save the table to create relationships.**

21. Repeat this process to turn the AgentID field into a lookup field that links to the agents table.

The columns are empty in the dialog box which asks you about lookup field column width (i.e., dialog box with *Hide key column* box) because you have not yet entered agent data. You will enter records in this table soon.

Table Validation Rules

Field validation rules allow you to specify the information allowed in a specific field. A field validation rule can only check the information entered in one field, but a table validation rule allows you to compare values from one field to another. For example, in the *TblTrips* table, both the departure date and return date fields will store trip dates. To help ensure that both dates are entered correctly (and not reversed), a simple validation rule might be to require that the return date occurs after the departure date.

In the next steps, you will create a table validation rule which requires that the return date occurs after the departure date.

1. In the Design View of *TblTrips*, notice if the *Properties Sheet* task pane appears on the right side of the screen.

2. If the task pane is not visible, right-click an empty area of the *Description* column and select *Properties* from the shortcut menu.

Under the *General* properties tab, notice *Validation Rule* and *Validation Text*. In the *Validation Rule* row you can specify the rule or condition for valid data in that field. The validation text is the message that Access displays when improper data is entered.

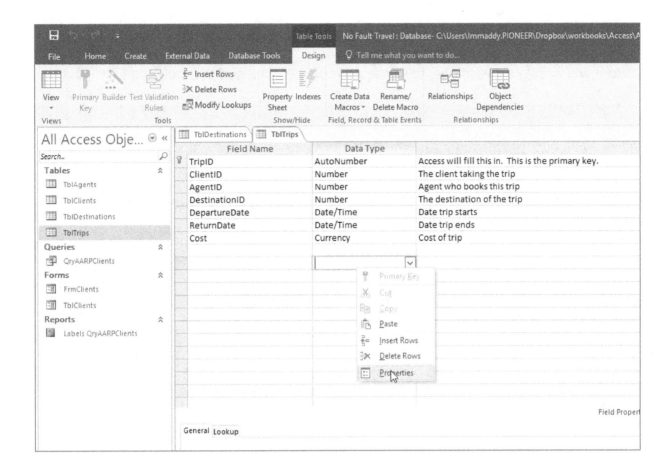

You can enter an expression (formula) to compare the return date and departure date.

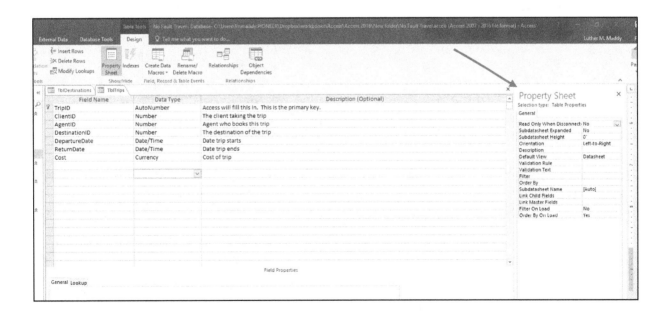

3. In the Validation Rule row type: *[DepartureDate]<[ReturnDate]*.

When you create expressions, field names must be enclosed in brackets [ ].

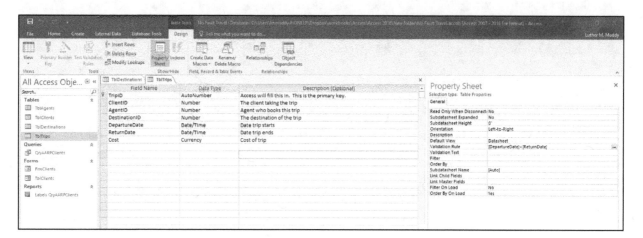

If you would like a larger viewable area to enter this rule, you can increase the size of the Table Properties task pane by dragging its left edge farther left. Alternatively, you can right click on the *Validation Rule* row and select *Zoom* from the shortcut menu.

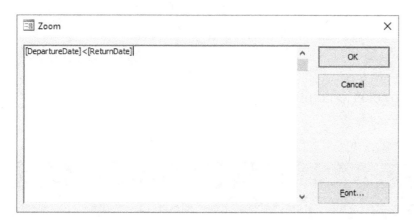

The expression, or formula you entered will cause Access to evaluate these two fields when a record is entered in the table. If the validation rule is not upheld, Access will display the error message contained in the *Validation Text* row.

4. In the Validation Text row type: *Check the return and departure dates.*

Property Sheet

×

Selection type: Table Properties

General

Read Only When Disconnect	No
Subdatasheet Expanded	No
Subdatasheet Height	0"
Orientation	Left-to-Right
Description	
Default View	Datasheet
Validation Rule	[DepartureDate] < [ReturnDate]
Validation Text	Check the return and departure dates.
Filter	
Order By	
Subdatasheet Name	[Auto]
Link Child Fields	
Link Master Fields	
Filter On Load	No
Order By On Load	Yes

5.   Save and close the table.

You should not have any records in the trips table. If you do, an error message may appear when you try to save the table. If this occurs, erase any records in this table and try the save command again.

6.   Close any other open tables.

Lesson #3: Working with Filters

In this lesson you will learn to:

Create and Use Filters

Lesson #3: Working with Filters

Filters provide a quick and easy way to view certain records in a table or form. A filter is a tool that performs some of the same functions as a query, but it is a separate object created in Access. With a simple mouse click to turn a filter on or off, you can switch between looking at a subset and the entire record set.

When you apply a filter, the word *Filtered* appears in the navigation bar (after the number of records) to indicate that you are looking at a filtered subset of records. Filters are very useful for doing simple record counts.

1.   Open the No Fault Travel database if it is not already open.

2.   Open *TblClients* in Datasheet View.

You can apply a filter by using the toolbar or right-clicking. In the next steps, you will use the right-click method.

3.   Right-click any cell where *Boise* occurs in the *City* field.

Filter by selection

You will now see a shortcut menu with several filter options. The *Equals "Boise"* option will instantly create a filter based on the text you have selected, Boise in this case.

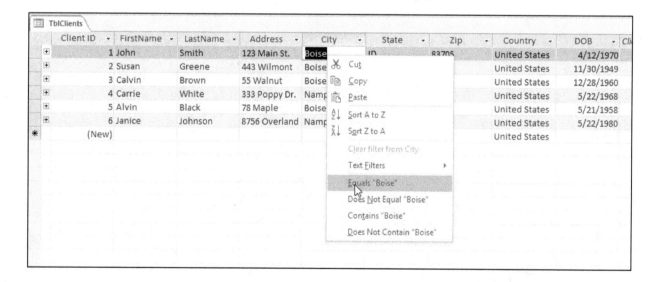

4.   In the shortcut menu, choose *Equals "Boise"*.

You should now only see the records with Boise in the city field. The navigation bar displays the number of records that meet this criterion and the word *Filtered* to indicate that a filter has been applied to the list of records you are viewing.

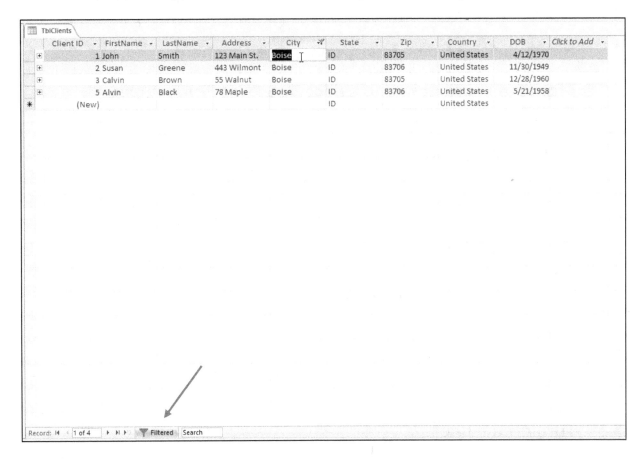

Removing a filter

After applying a filter you will eventually want to return to the unfiltered record set. The *Toggle Filter* tool on the ribbon will cause Access to toggle between the unfiltered and filtered record sets.

1.   **Locate and click the *Toggle Filter* tool on the ribbon to turn the filter off.**

You should now see all the records in the table. The navigation bar should also display *Unfiltered*.

Filter Excluding Selection

In the previous steps, you used the *Equals* option to show all the records which have that value in the field. Access also allows you to filter all records which do not match the value you have selected with the *Does Not Equal* option.

1.   Right-click on Boise in any cell in the *City* field.

2.   From the shortcut menu, select *Does Not Equal "Boise."*

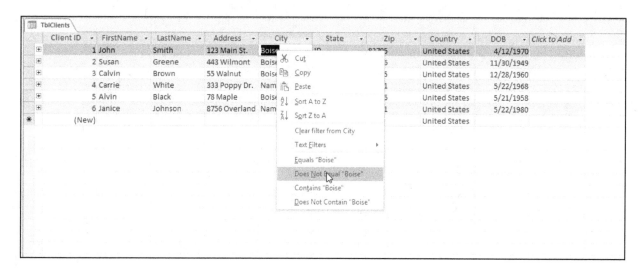

You should now see all the records which do not have Boise in the *City* field.

3.   Turn off the filter.

You can also easily turn off a filter by clicking on the *Filtered* indicator on the navigation bar.

Using multiple criteria in filters

Similar to queries, you can impose filter criteria on more than one field. You can add a filter(s) to filtered record sets or use a feature called *Filter By Form*. We will explore both options.

1.   In the Datasheet View, right-click Boise in the *City* field and use the *Equals* option to view only the records with Boise.

The records for Boise should be listed as they were earlier. Now apply a second filter to the filtered set of records. In other words, you will apply a second condition, but to only those records with Boise in the *City* field.

2. **Viewing the filtered records in the table, right-click 83705 in the *Zip* field and choose the *Equals 83705* filter option.**

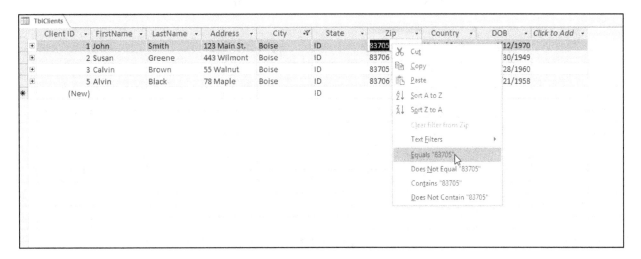

Only the records with Boise in the *City* field and the zip code 83705 in the *Zip* field are displayed. This example shows that you can use multiple filters to further narrow the record set.

3. **Turn off both filters by clicking the *Filtered* indicator on the navigation bar.**

We will now use the *Filter By Form* option to filter with more than one criteria.

4. **Click the *Advanced* tool in the *Sort & Filter* group and select *Filter By Form*.**

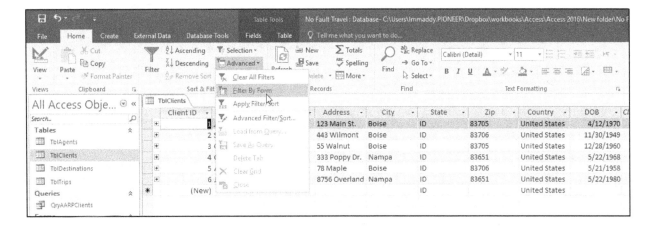

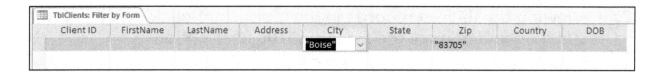

The *Filter by Form* window appears with the last applied criteria. You can modify and delete criteria using this form. You can apply filters to multiple fields.

5.   In the *Filter by Form* window, delete the criteria in both the City and Zip fields.

To delete existing criteria you can highlight the criteria and then press the (Delete) key.

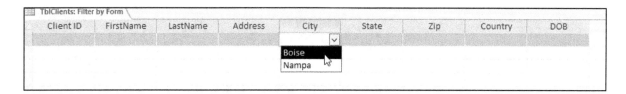

6.   In the *Filter by Form* window, click the dropdown arrow in the *City* field and choose *Boise*.

Using the *Filter by Form* option makes it easy to specify criteria in multiple fields. It also allows you to use comparison operators such as > or < in filters. You will now use a comparison operator to add a criterion to the date of birth field.

You may also notice that Access added hashtags (#) to the date and quotation marks (") to the city. These symbols indicate that Access recognizes the date as numeric and the city as text.

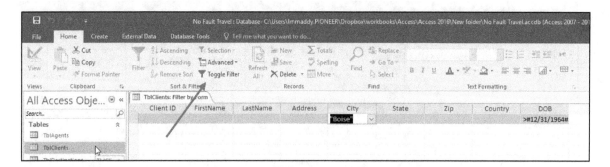

7.   Click in the *DOB* field and type >12/31/1964. Click the *Toggle Filter* tool.

You should see a list of the clients who live in Boise and were born after 1964.

8.   Click the Toggle Filter tool to view all records.

Using filters in forms

You can also use the filter by selection option when viewing records in a form. This is different than the *Filter by Form* option we just explored. In the next steps, you will apply a filter in a form. You will also add some additional records.

1.   Close the clients table and open the clients form, *FrmClients*.

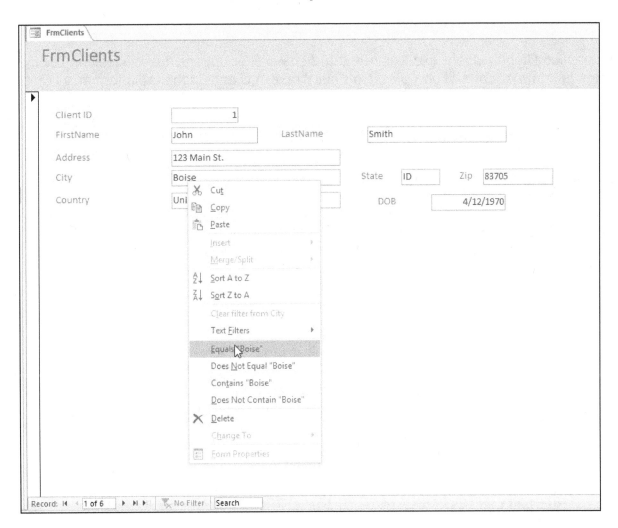

2.   In the first record, right-click *Boise* in the *City* field and choose *Equals Boise* in the shortcut menu.

3.   Scroll through the records.

Notice that only the records for clients in Boise are displayed. Look at the navigation bar. The *filtered* indicator appears and only four records are included. You are viewing records with a filter applied.

4.   Use the form to enter the following two additional records.

Maria Gomez 453 Blaine Caldwell, ID 83605 9/21/1969	Roger McFadden 4423 Cleveland Caldwell, ID 83605 5/21/1980

We applied filtering in forms to illustrate that Access filter options are available in both tables and forms. You will now view No Fault Travel's clients in the table format.

5.   Close *FrmClients* and open the clients table, *TblClients*.

Using "containing" in filters

In the previous exercises, the filters set criteria for the entire value in a field. However, it is also possible to set criteria for just a portion of the field. For example, you may want to find the records of clients who live on an avenue. In this case you would filter the *Address* field with a filter *Containing "Ave."* These filters are not case sensitive.

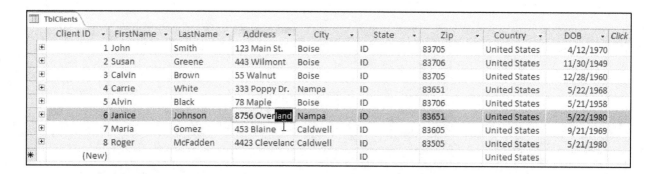

Client ID	FirstName	LastName	Address	City	State	Zip	Country	DOB	Click
1 John		Smith	123 Main St.	Boise	ID	83705	United States	4/12/1970	
2 Susan		Greene	443 Wilmont	Boise	ID	83706	United States	11/30/1949	
3 Calvin		Brown	55 Walnut	Boise	ID	83705	United States	12/28/1960	
4 Carrie		White	333 Poppy Dr.	Nampa	ID	83651	United States	5/22/1968	
5 Alvin		Black	78 Maple	Boise	ID	83706	United States	5/21/1958	
6 Janice		Johnson	8756 Overland	Nampa	ID	83651	United States	5/22/1980	
7 Maria		Gomez	453 Blaine	Caldwell	ID	83605	United States	9/21/1969	
8 Roger		McFadden	4423 Clevelanc	Caldwell	ID	83505	United States	5/21/1980	
(New)					ID		United States		

1.   Carefully select only *land* in the *Address* field for Janice Johnson.

Instead of accessing filter options by right-clicking to open the shortcut menu as we did earlier, we will use filter tools on the ribbon in the next steps. Either method can be used.

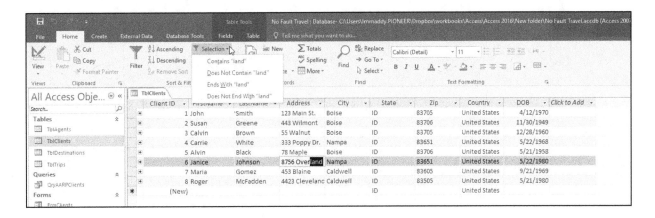

2. **Then click the *Selection* tool in the *Sort & Filter* group and choose the *Contains "land"* option.**

Notice the *Ends With "land"* and *Does Not End With "land"* options available for filtering. If you had instead selected *875* in this cell, filter options would have included *Begins With 875* and *Does Not Begin With 875*.

Once the *Contains "land"* filter option is applied, only the records whose *Address* field contains "land" will be listed.

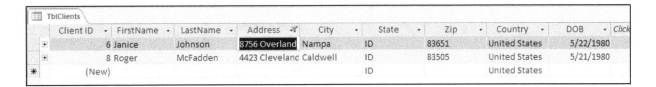

3. **Toggle the filter to turn it off. Close the clients table. Click *No* in the dialog box which asks if you want to save the changes to the design of the table.**

If you had saved the table design changes, the last filter you applied, *Contains "land"*, would have been stored as part of the table information. In that case, the next time you opened the clients table, you could apply that filter by simply clicking the *Toggle Filter* tool.

4. **Close the database.**

Lesson #4: Changing Join Properties

In this lesson you will learn to:

Change Join Properties in Queries

Lesson #4: Working with Join Properties

Working with related tables in queries

When you create queries based on related tables, even though you do not specify any criteria, you will only see the records that are related in each of the tables. For instance, with this database, if you created a query based on *TblClients* and *TblTrips*, you would only see the clients who had scheduled trips. If a client had taken more than one trip, that client would show up more than once in the result of the query.

Currently, there are no records in the trips table. If you created a query based on both the trips and clients tables, there would be no records in the query. In the next steps, we will add some records, so we can see how queries and related tables work.

1. **If it is not already open, open the No Fault Travel database. Open *TblAgents* in Datasheet View.**

2. **Enter the records shown below in the travel agents table.**

TblAgents				
AgentID ▾	FName ▾	LName ▾	Commission ▾	Click to Add ▾
1	Susie	Jackson	2.00%	
2	Matthew	Anderson	4.00%	
3	Ramona	Martinez	5.00%	
4	Carl	Lee	3.00%	
* (New)			0.00%	

3. **Close TblAgents. Open TblTrips.**

In the next step, you will enter trip information in the trips table. In Lesson 2, we created lookup fields in this table for the *ClientID*, *AgentID*, and *DestinationID* fields. For these fields, you will simply select the information from a dropdown list so data entry is easier!

4. **Enter the records in the trips table as shown below.**

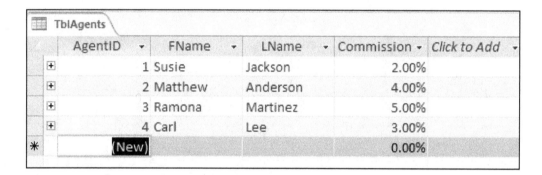

TblTrips							
TripID ▾	ClientID ▾	AgentID ▾	DestinationID ▾	DepartureDa ▾	ReturnDate ▾	Cost ▾	Click to Add ▾
1	Susan	Carl	Maui	7/16/2018	7/26/2018	$2,500.00	
2	Janice	Carl	London	6/5/2018	7/4/2018	$3,950.00	
3	John	Ramona	New York	8/30/2018	9/13/2018	$6,500.00	
4	Susan	Susie	Hanoi	10/18/2018	10/25/2018	$4,980.00	
* (New)						$0.00	

You will see a list of names in the *ClientID* and the *AgentID* fields. Please recall that we designed the lookup fields to show names in the dropdown lists, but the fields actually store the client and agent identification numbers.

5.   **Close the trips table. Create a new query using the *Query Design* tool.**

6.   **In this query, add *TblClients* and *TblTrips*. Add the fields: *FirstName*, *LastName*, *DestinationID*, *DepartureDate*, *ReturnDate*, and *Cost*.**

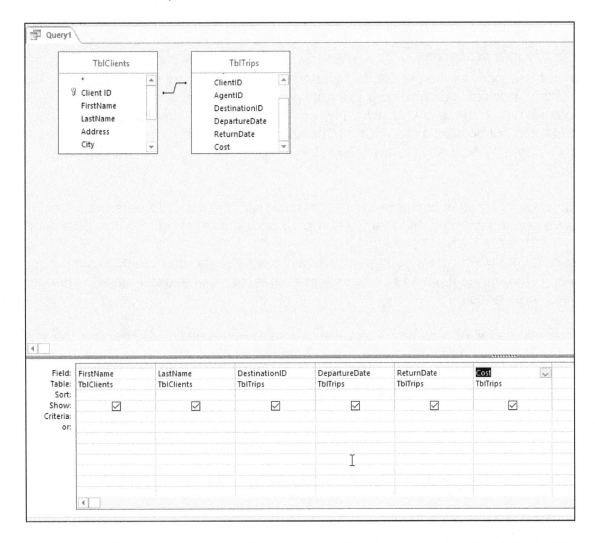

The join line between the two tables indicates that they are related or linked. This relationship was created when the lookup field in *TblTrips* was created in Lesson 2.

6.   **View the results of this query.**

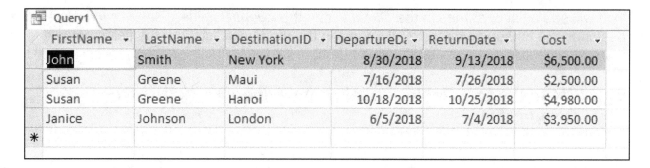

You can see that only three clients' names appear in this query. There are eight clients (records) in *TblClients* but only the clients who have booked trips appear in the query results. Susan Greene appears twice -- once for each trip she has booked.

Changing the join properties

Assume that you work for the No Fault Travel agency and you want to increase the number of trips booked. After running this query, you realize that some "clients" have never booked a trip. These clients probably requested information from No Fault Travel, but have not booked a trip. From a marketing standpoint, these people are potential customers because they are interested in travel and you have their contact information.

You could simply manually compare the clients table with the query to determine which clients have not booked trips, but manual comparison is not practical for large data sets.

The best solution is to create a query which lists the clients who do not appear in the trips table. This query will have to be based on both tables, but you will have to change how records are chosen.

The *join* properties tell Access which records to display in the query. By default, the join properties only show the records that occur in both tables. But you can change the join properties to have Access show you all the records from either table. Then you can set criteria so that the query show only the records of clients who have not scheduled a trip.

This is a long explanation and the good news is that actually changing the join properties is probably easier than understanding why you would want to change them.

1.   Return to the Design View of the query.

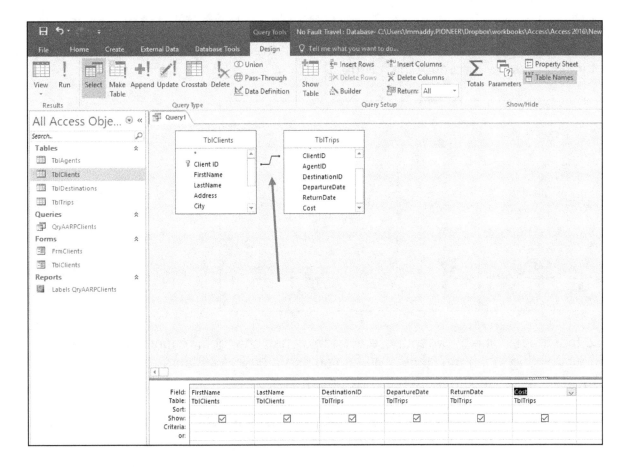

2. Carefully double-click the join line between *TblClients* and *TblTrips*.

You should now see the Join Properties dialog box. Here you can change how the query treats related records.

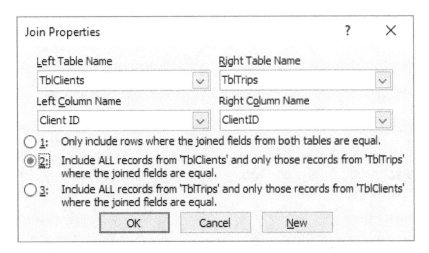

3. In the Join Properties dialog box, choose the second option, *"Include All records from TblClients..."* and click OK.

This option tells Access to display all the records in the clients table, whether or not the trips table contains a record for that client.

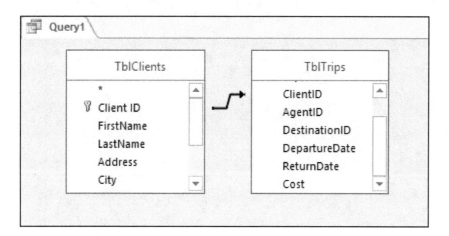

Notice that the join line between these two tables has changed in appearance. There is an arrow pointing to the trips table. When you see a query with an arrow in the join line, you should realize the join properties have been altered.

4. View the results of this query with the join properties changed.

FirstName	LastName	DestinationID	DepartureDate	ReturnDate	Cost
John	Smith	New York	8/30/2018	9/13/2018	$6,500.00
Susan	Greene	Maui	7/16/2018	7/26/2018	$2,500.00
Susan	Greene	Hanoi	10/18/2018	10/25/2018	$4,980.00
Calvin	Brown				
Carrie	White				
Alvin	Black				
Janice	Johnson	London	6/5/2018	7/4/2018	$3,950.00
Maria	Gomez				
Roger	McFadden				

Notice that all clients are now displayed. The next step is to set criteria to show only those clients who have not booked a trip.

5. **Return to the Design View of this query. In the *Criteria* row of the *DestinationID* field column, type *is null*.**

6. **Delete the *DepartureDate*, *ReturnDate*, and *Cost* fields from the query. Add the *Address*, *City*, *State*, and *Zip* fields from *TblClients*. Uncheck the *Show* checkbox for the *DestinationID* field.**

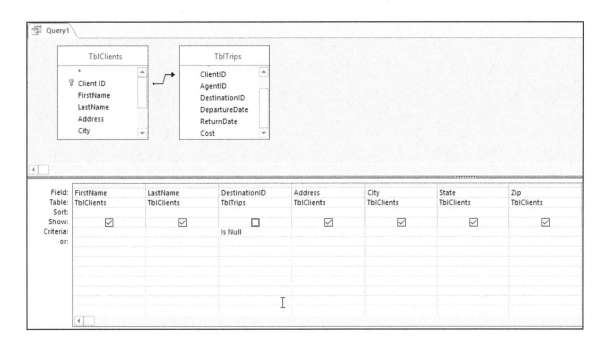

7. **View the results of this query.**

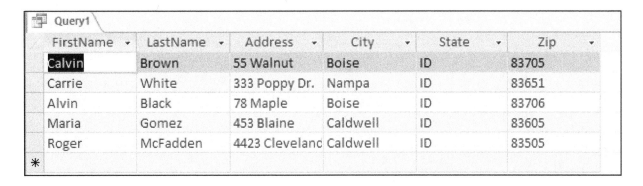

You now have the names and addresses of individuals in *TblClients* who have never booked a trip.

8. **Save this query as *QryClientsWithoutTrips* and close it.**

Lesson #5: Creating Calculations in Queries

In this lesson you will learn to:

Create Calculated Fields in Queries
Use the Totaling Feature in Queries

Lesson #5: Working with Calculations in Queries

Access allows users to easily create calculations within queries, forms, or reports. Computations are most often within queries because a calculated field in a query can be used in multiple reports or forms as needed. In this lesson you will create calculated fields in queries, reports, and forms.

1.   Open the No Fault Travel database, if it is not already open.

2.   On the Create tab, click the *Query Design* tool to create a new query based on *TblAgents* and *TblTrips*.

3.   Add the fields: *AgentID*, *LName*, *FName*, *DepartureDate*, *DestinationID*, *Cost* and *CommissionRate*.

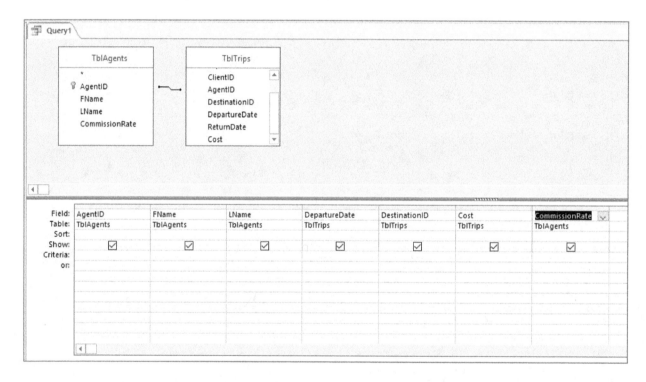

Recall that you created the *DestinationID* field as a lookup field. Destination options are displayed in a dropdown list, but the destination's identification number is stored in the field.

Creating computed fields in a query

To create calculations within a query, go to a blank column because you are creating a new field. In the top cell for field name, type the name of the new field, but do not press enter. After the field name, type a colon (:) and then the formula. In Access formulas, field names must be enclosed in brackets [ ]. For example, the following text would create a calculated field *Length*, which computes the difference between two date fields.

Length:[date1]-[date2]

In the next steps, you will create a new field *Commission* which will compute how much the agent earned in commission for each trip booked.

1.   In the blank column just after the *CommissionRate* field, click in the *Field* row. Right-click to open the shortcut menu and select *Zoom*.

Using the Zoom dialog box makes typing longer formulas easier because it provides a larger visible window. Earlier, we used the shortcut keys (Shift+F2) to open the Zoom dialog box.

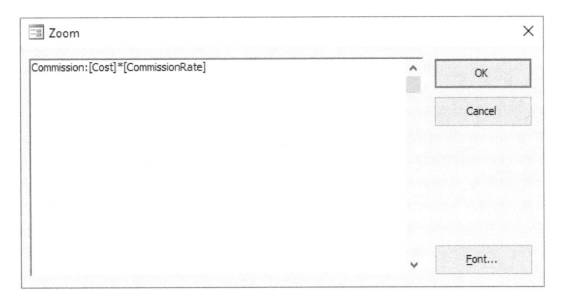

2.   In the Zoom dialog box, type the following expression and then click OK: *Commission:[Cost]*[CommissionRate]*.

Expressions are not case sensitive, so upper or lower case does not matter. However, spelling does! Be sure to spell the field names exactly as they are appear in the table.

3.   View the results of this query.

AgentID	FName	LName	DepartureD:	DestinationID	Cost	Commission	Commission
1	Susie	Jackson	10/18/2018	Hanoi	$4,980.00	2.00%	99.6
3	Ramona	Martinez	8/30/2018	New York	$6,500.00	5.00%	325
4	Carl	Lee	7/16/2018	Maui	$2,500.00	3.00%	75
4	Carl	Lee	6/5/2018	London	$3,950.00	3.00%	118.5
(New)							

You should see the new field *Commission* and its computed values. Next, you will add currency formatting to the field to improve its appearance.

4.   Return to Design View of this query.

5.   Right-click in the *Field* row of the *Commission* field. Choose *Properties* on the shortcut menu.

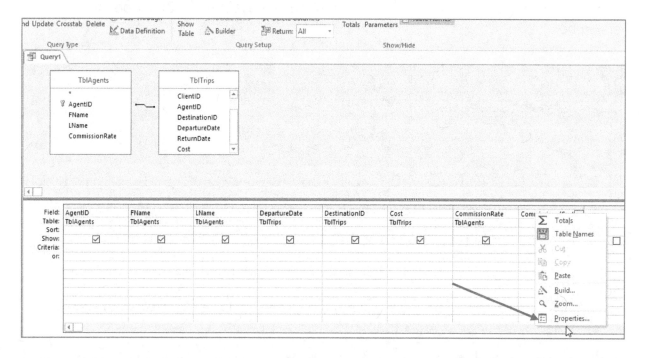

The Property Sheet task pane should open. (We used this earlier to create table validation rules.) The text *Selection type: Field Properties* appears just under the *Property Sheet* title on the task pane; this lets you know that only the properties for one field can be modified and not the entire table because a specific field was selected.

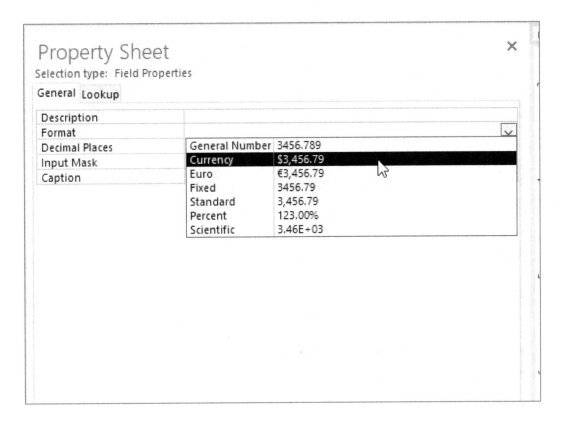

6. In the *Format* row of the Property Sheet, click the dropdown arrow and choose *Currency*. Close the Property Sheet.

7. Save this query as *QryCommissionsPaid* and then run it again.

Now the commission field should be formatted in currency format.

8. **Close the query.**

Since this calculated field was created within a query, it is available in any forms or reports based on this query. It can even be used in another query if it is based on this query.

Using functions in queries

Microsoft Access has many built-in functions which can be used in expressions for fields created within queries, reports or forms. The functions in Access are clearly divided into different categories including Date/Time, Financial, Math, and Text. Built-in functions simplify creating complex expressions in Access, just like they do in Excel.

In the next steps, you will use the Month() function to determine each client's birth month. Computing the birth month makes generating a list of clients with a birthday in a particular month easier. Many companies send customers birthday greetings or special discounts during the month of their birthdays.

The syntax for this date function and all Access functions is: Month([DOB]). All functions require parenthesis ( ), which identifies them as functions (rather than fields) in expressions. Also, note the brackets around the field *DOB*. Field names are always included in brackets [ ], even when used inside functions.

1. **On the Create tab, select the *Query Design* tool to create a new query based on *TblClients*. Add all the fields except *ClientID* to the query grid.**

2. **Save this query as *QryClientBirthMonth* but stay in Design View.**

To be used in the Expression Builder, queries must be saved with their default name. You will save the query again once you have completed it.

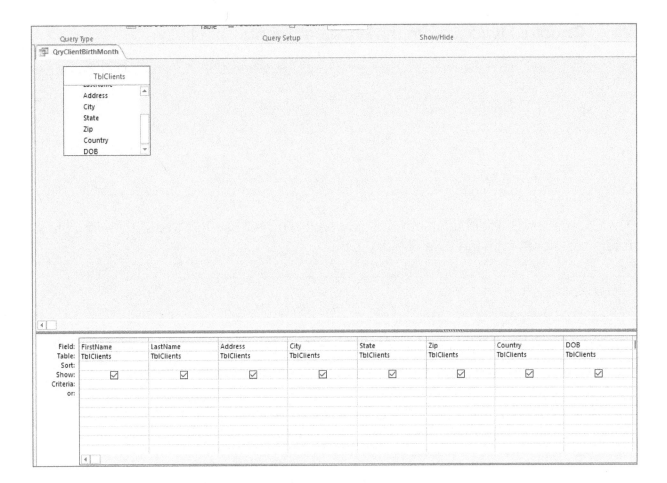

Using the Expression Builder

When creating complex expressions, especially those that use functions, Access provides the *Expression Builder* to make creating them easier. The Expression Builder provides a list of all available functions. The Expression Builder is typically opened by right-clicking and choosing *Build…* on the shortcut menu.

In the next steps, you will use the Expression Builder to create a calculated field which lists the birth month of each client. This value can be used to select clients by birth month.

1.   **In the empty column next to the *DOB* field, right-click in the *Field* row.**

2. Choose *Build*... from the shortcut menu.

The Expression Builder dialog box should open. You will use this to build the formula to return the month from the date of birth field.

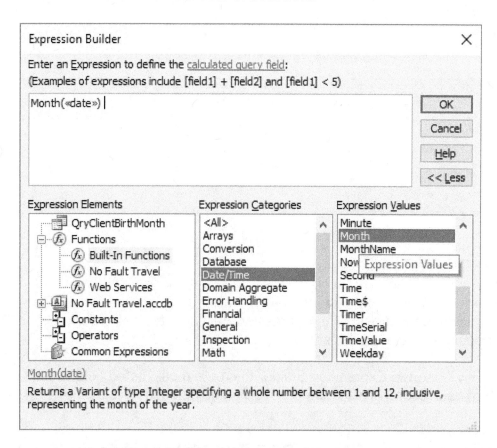

3. In the Expression Builder dialog box, locate and double-click *Functions* in the left column.

Double-clicking expands the functions folder to allow you to choose from Access' built-in functions or functions specific to this database. Specific functions are created through VBA programming and we have not yet created any specific functions for this database. We will do that in a more advanced course.

4.   **When the Functions folder expands, click once on *Built-In Functions.***

In the middle column, *Expression Categories*, you can now choose the type of function you would like to use.

5.   **Click once on the *Date/Time* category in the middle column.**

The date/time functions should appear in the right column, *Expression Values*.

6.   **Scroll down and double-click the *Month* function in the right column.**

In the text box used to enter the expression for the calculated field, *Month(<<date>>)* should appear. The text *<<date>>* indicates that Access wants you to insert the date field inside the *Month()* function.

7.   **In the expression, click once on <<*date*>> to select it.**

In the next steps, you will replace *<<date>>* with the field you wish to use to return the month. First you will select the query which contains the field you want to use and then you will select the field.

8.   **In the left column *Expression Elements*, click once on *QryClientBirthMonth* to select it.**

A list of fields in the query should appear in the middle column, *Expression Categories*.

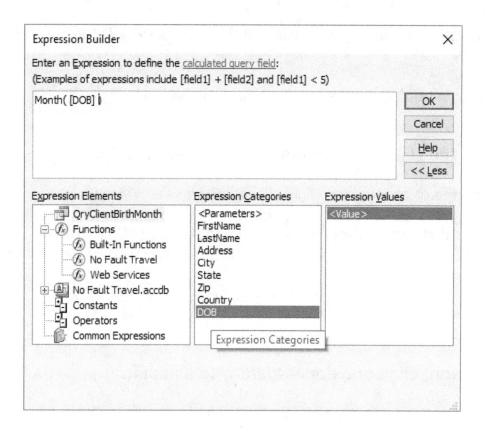

9. In the middle column, double-click the *DOB* field and click OK.

The completed expression should appear in the text area. You could have also manually typed the field name in the expression as long as you had spelled it correctly and enclosed it in brackets.

10. View the results of this query.

The last column, named by default *Expr1*, should display the month number from each client's birthdate. In an earlier portion of the lesson, we named a calculated field and provided an expression for it in the *Field* row. When we clicked on the *Field* row in the empty column to create a field for the birth month, we could have named it before we used the Expression Builder. Since we did not provide a name, Access named it *Expr1*. Now, let's give this field a meaningful name.

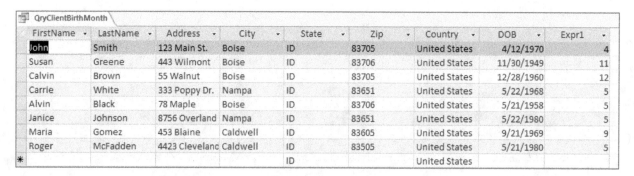

FirstName	LastName	Address	City	State	Zip	Country	DOB	Expr1
John	Smith	123 Main St.	Boise	ID	83705	United States	4/12/1970	4
Susan	Greene	443 Wilmont	Boise	ID	83706	United States	11/30/1949	11
Calvin	Brown	55 Walnut	Boise	ID	83705	United States	12/28/1960	12
Carrie	White	333 Poppy Dr.	Nampa	ID	83651	United States	5/22/1968	5
Alvin	Black	78 Maple	Boise	ID	83706	United States	5/21/1958	5
Janice	Johnson	8756 Overland	Nampa	ID	83651	United States	5/22/1980	5
Maria	Gomez	453 Blaine	Caldwell	ID	83605	United States	9/21/1969	9
Roger	McFadden	4423 Cleveland	Caldwell	ID	83505	United States	5/21/1980	5
*				ID		United States		

11. **Return to Design View. Click in the *Field* row of *Expr1*. Open the *Zoom* dialog box from the shortcut menu or by pressing (Shift+F2).**

12. **In the Zoom dialog box, change *Expr1* to *BirthMonth* and click OK.**

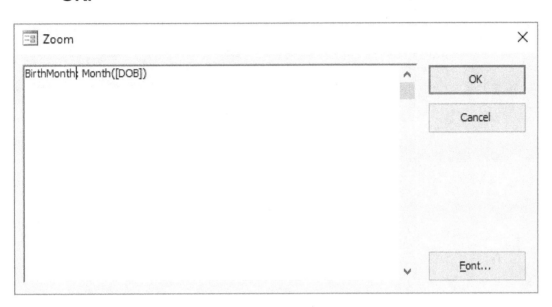

13. **View the results of this query again.**

Now the calculated field should have a recognizable purpose, which makes referring to it in a form or report much easier.

14. **Save and close this query.**

Creating Totaling Queries

Assume that you would like to know how much each travel agent has been paid in commissions. One way to get this information would be to create a report that totals the commissions paid for each travel agent. But an easier method would be to create a totaling query. Totaling queries compute sums, averages and other statistics for numeric fields. You have the option of computing these values individually or as a grouped total.

In our case, the grouping field will be travel agent since you want the values computed for each agent. In this portion of the lesson, we will use Access' totaling feature to calculate statistics for each travel agent's commissions.

1.   On the Create tab, click *Query Design*.

Creating a query based on a query

Up to this point, we have created queries based on tables. However in the next steps, each agent's total commission will be based on a calculated field you created in the *QryCommissionsPaid* query to compute the commission for each trip.

You can create the totaling query with the names of the travel agents and the commission for each trip.

1.   In the Show Table dialog box, click the *Queries* tab, add *QryCommissionsPaid* and then close the Show Table dialog box.

2.   Add the fields *Lname, Fname,* and *Commission* to the Query Grid.

You will be grouping by the agent's name and computing the total commissions earned for each agent.

To do summary computations in an Access query, use the *Totals* tool on the ribbon. This will add a new row in the Query Grid that will allow you to either choose *Group By* or to compute a summary calculation.

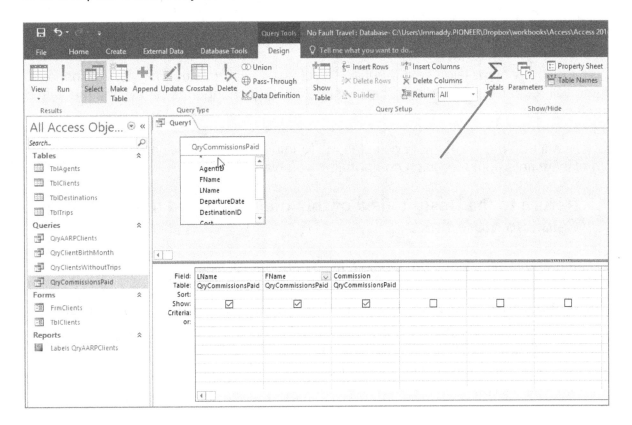

3.   **Click the *Totals* tool in the Show/Hide group.**

Notice that a new row, *Total*, has been added to the Query Grid. Here is where you specify whether the field is a grouping field or should be a calculation.

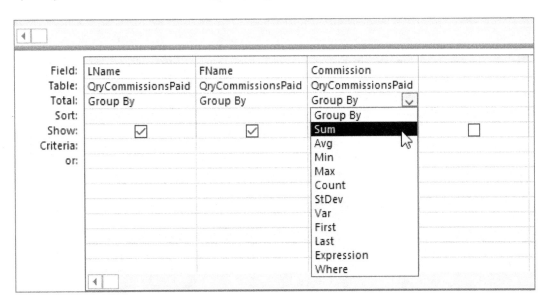

4.   In the *Commission* field column, click in the *Total* row. From the dropdown list, choose *Sum*.

5.   **View the results of this query.**

Notice the total commission field for each travel agent. Increasing the width of the last column will reveal its title, *SumOfCommission*. We will change the name and the field's formatting later.

First, we will add more summary calculations to this query. You will need to add the *Commission* field again for each computation you want.

6.   **Return to the Design View of this query and add the *Commission* field two more times.**

You can quickly add a field from the field list by double-clicking.

7.   **Change the computation for the second *Commission* field to *Avg* and change the third *Commission* field to *Count*.**

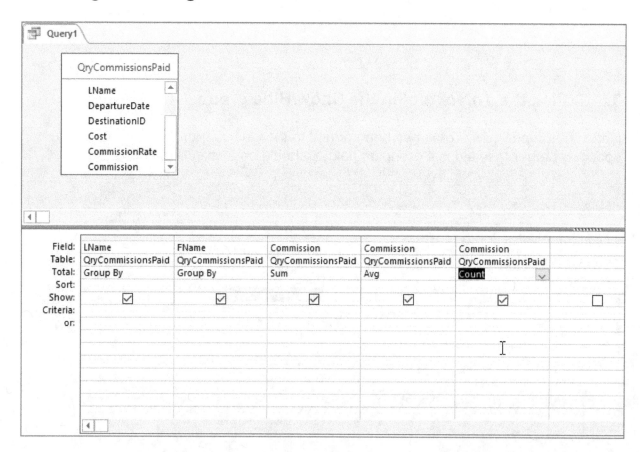

You have now told Access to compute the total (sum), average, and the number of commissions for each travel agent.

8.   View the results of this query to verify that it computes the two additional statistics.

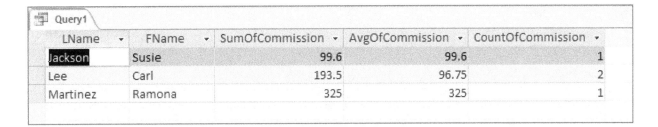

Changing field captions

The names of the calculated fields may not be what you want for later reference. Access allows you to change the field name that the query displays by changing the field's caption property. In this portion of the lesson, you will change the caption and formatting options for the computed fields.

9.   Return to the Design View of this query.

10.   Display the properties by right-clicking in the *Field* row for the *SumOfCommission* field.

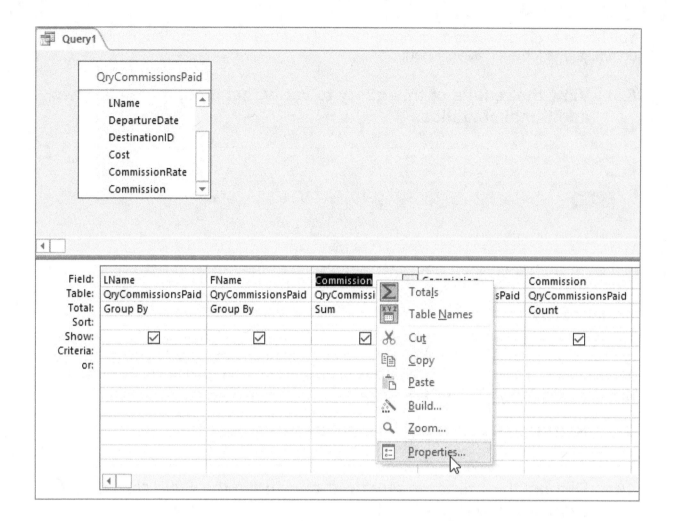

11. Change the *Format* property to *Currency*. In the *Caption* property, type *Total Commissions*. Close the Property Sheet.

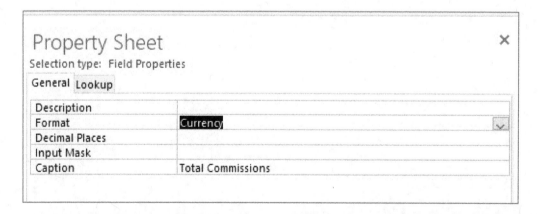

12. In the Average column, change the format property to currency and the caption to *Average Commission*.

13. In the Count column, change the caption to *# of trips booked*.

The format property should not be changed to currency because the number of booked trips is an integer number, not a dollar amount.

14. **View the results of this query. Change the column widths as needed to view the new captions.**

LName ▾	FName ▾	Total Commissions ▾	Average Commission ▾	# of trips booked ▾
Jackson	Susie	$99.60	$99.60	1
Lee	Carl	$193.50	$96.75	2
Martinez	Ramona	$325.00	$325.00	1

15. **Save this query as *QryAgentCommissionStatistics* and then close it.**

Lesson #6: Advanced Form Features

In this lesson you will learn to:

Create Calculated Fields in Forms
Create and Use Sub-Forms

Lesson #6: Advanced Form Features

1.   If it is not already open, open the No Fault Travel database.

2.   Use the form wizard to create a form based on all the fields in *TblTrips*. Choose a *Tabular* form layout. Name the form *FrmTrips*.

3.   Modify the labels and text boxes so the form appears as the one below in Design View.

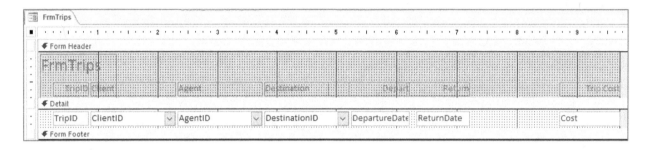

Remember not to change the text in the text boxes. The text boxes must refer to the fields in the table. Use the ruler shown in the image as a guide. Increase the size of the text boxes to properly display the dates. You will use the blank space between the return date and cost field to add a calculated field in the next portion of this lesson.

4.   View the form in Form View. Make sure it resembles the one below.

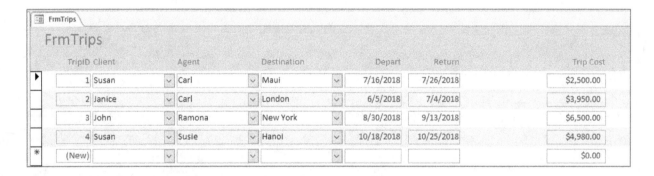

5.   **Return to Design View of this form.**

We will now add a calculated field to this form. Ideally, most calculations should be performed in a query so they can be used, if desired, in multiple forms or queries. However, if you only need to use a calculated field on one form or one report, Access allows you to do this.

Creating a new text box

To create a field that computes values in a form you will need to create a new text box. This text box, instead of being bound to a field in the table or query, will compute a value based on the expression you enter into it.

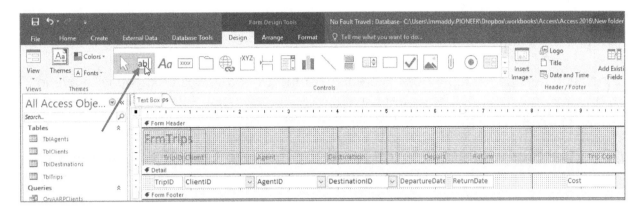

6. Locate and click the Text Box tool in the Controls group.

When you create a text box using the Controls, the text box will appear at the location of the mouse pointer when you click. The label will appear to the left of the text box (in columnar form, not tabular). You will need to move the label and resize and position the text box.

7. Move the mouse pointer just to the right of the *ReturnDate* text box and click.

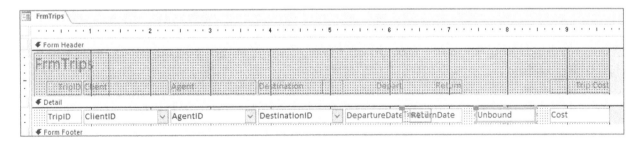

A new text box containing the text "*Unbound*" should appear where you clicked the mouse. A label for this text box should also appear to the left of the text box.

8. **Carefully click on and then delete the label for the new text box.**

9. **If needed, reposition the *Unbound* text box so if fits nicely between the text boxes for the return date and cost fields.**

To achieve more uniform spacing if desired, you can also move the trip cost label and text box to the left.

Since you deleted the label Access created for the *Unbound* text box, you will have to add one yourself. Simply copy the existing label for trip cost. After copying it, you will need to reposition it and change the text it displays.

10. **Carefully select just the label for the *Trip Cost* field and click the *Copy* tool on the Home tab.**

The copy and paste commands can also be executed by using the shortcut keys Control+C and Control+V or by right-clicking to open the shortcut menu.

11. **Now execute the *Paste* command and move the copy of the label above the *Unbound* text box.**

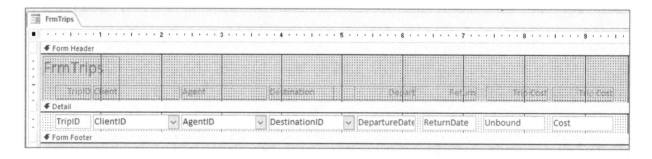

You may need to change the size of the *Form Header*. If so, you can click and drag the top of the *Detail* bar to shorten the *Form Header*.

12. **Change the text on the copied label to read *Trip Length*.**

You will now enter a formula into the text box to compute the length of the trip.

Entering formulas in a text box

To have a text box compute a value, you must enter a formula into the control source of that box. While you can simply click in the text box and type the formula, you will often want to do this using the *Property Sheet* for the text box. Since you may also want to change the format of the computed value to, for example, currency, you will need to change the box's properties eventually. When creating a formula using the *Property Sheet*, you enter the formula in the *Control Source* row, located on the *Data* tab.

1. Select the *Unbound* text box and display its properties.

Text box properties can be accessed using the ribbon or shortcut menu. On the ribbon's *Design* tab, the *Property Sheet* tool is located in the Tools group. You can also right-click the text box and choose *Properties* from the shortcut menu.

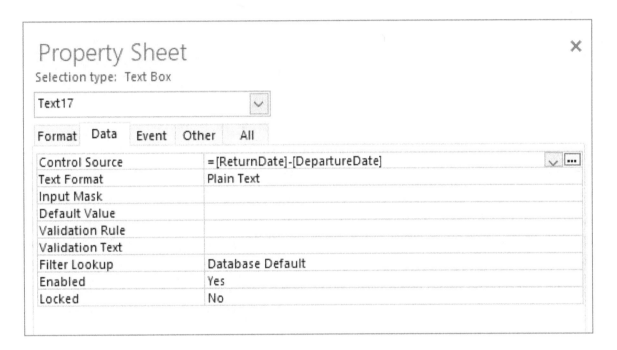

2. On the Property Sheet, display the *Data* tab. In the *Control Source* row, type =[ReturnDate]-[DepartureDate].

Notice this formula begins with an equals sign. The equals sign is needed for form and report calculations, but not for calculated fields in queries.

Instead of typing this formula in the space provided on the row, you could also use the *Zoom* dialog box or the *Expression Builder* dialog box to enter the formula, as we did earlier. Expression Builder will open when you click the build ![build] button in the row. The Zoom box can be opened with the shortcut keys (Shift+F2). Alternatively, either dialog box can be accessed by right-clicking in the *Control Source* row to open the shortcut menu.

3.   Click the *Format* tab in the Property Sheet and change the *Format* property to *General Number*.

4.   Close the Property Sheet and save the form. View the form in Form View.

You should see the trip length computed in the calculated field you created.

5.   Close the *FrmTrips* form after examining it.

Creating and using subforms

When you created the lookup fields in the trips table, Access created relationships between the trips table and the destinations, clients, and agents tables. To view the relationships between tables, go to the *Database Tools* tab on the ribbon and click on the *Relationships* tool.

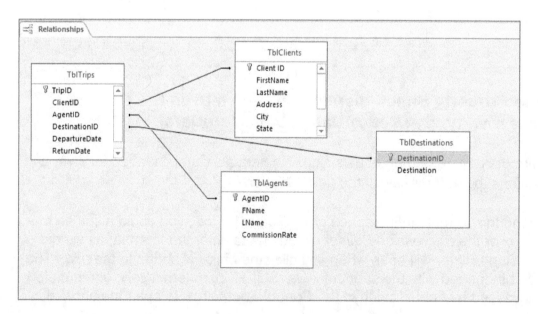

If you use the *Form* tool to create a new form from one of the tables linked to *TblTrips*, the new form will display fields from the table you selected and the linked records in the trips table. In the next step, you will create a form based on the agents table.

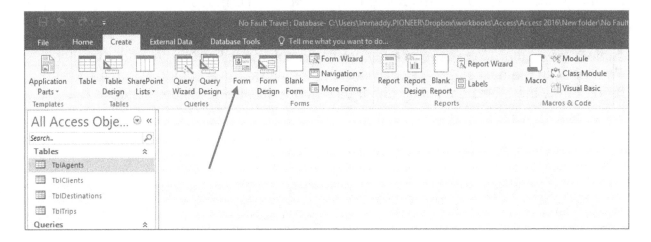

1.   **In the navigation pane, click once on *TblAgents*. On the Create tab, click the *Form* tool.**

You should see a main form for *TblAgents* and a subform with the linked table *TblTrips*.

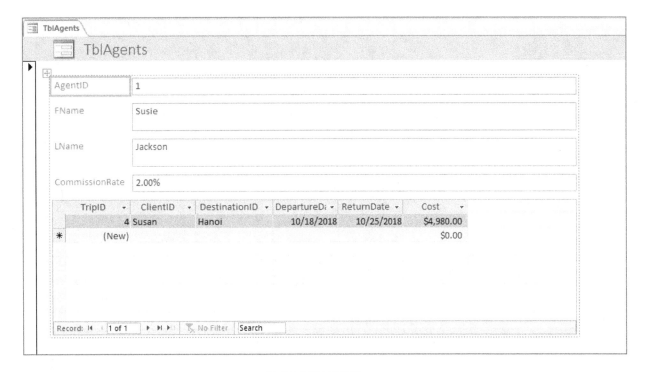

2.   **Save this new form as *FrmAgents* and close it.**

If existing forms are based on related records, you can combine them using the *subform* feature. Forms can have more than one subform. For example, if you added a payment history table to this database, you could add a subform to the clients form that displayed the trip information and another subform for payment information.

When creating forms with subforms, the main form should be columnar and the subform(s) tabular. You have already created a columnar *FrmClients* and a tabular *FrmTrips*. In the next steps, we will insert the trips form (as a subform) into the clients form. Since the tables are linked, the trips that are displayed will be related to the current client record.

3.   Display *FrmClients* in Design View.

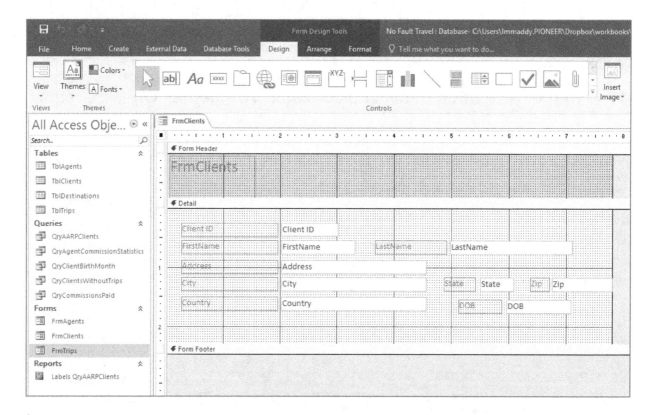

4.   Carefully drag *FrmTrips* from the Navigation Pane to the bottom left corner of *FrmClient* (below the *Country* field).

In the clients form, notice a large control which will be the list of trips booked by the client.

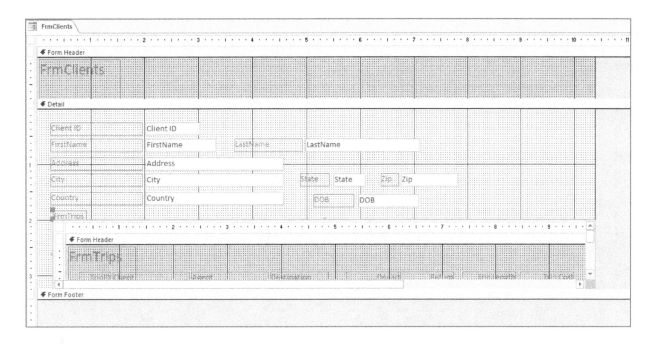

5. Increase the height of the *FrmTrips* subform by approximately 1."

You might have to first increase the height of the *FrmClients* form by dragging the *Form Footer* bar down slightly, so that you can see the bottom center sizing handle on the *FrmTrips* subform.

6. Save and then switch to Form View.

The client and the trips booked by that client should be visible. To browse through the client records, use the navigation buttons at the bottom of the clients form window. The navigation buttons for the trips are located on the trips subform.

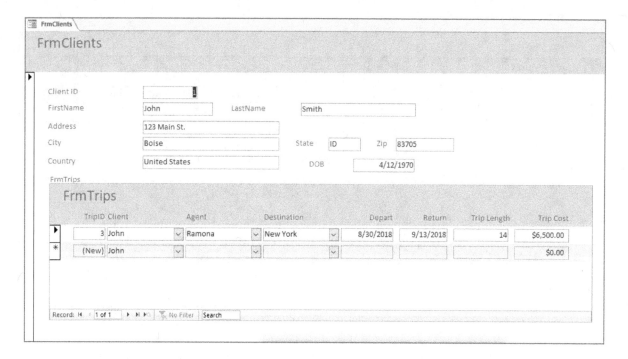

7. **Display Carrie White's record and enter an additional trip as shown below.**

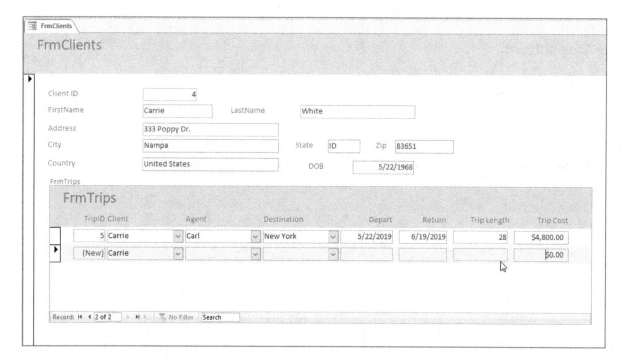

This client can be found by browsing through the records using the navigation buttons or using the *Find* tool on the ribbon's Home tab. As you can see from this portion of the lesson, subforms are a convenient way to enter and edit data.

8. **Close the Clients form.**

Lesson #7: Advanced Report Features

In this lesson you will learn to:

Create Calculations in Reports
Control Page Breaks
Concatenate Text Fields

Lesson #7: Advanced Report Features

Calculations in reports

The procedure for creating calculated fields in reports is similar to the process of creating computed fields in forms. To create a new field in a report, create a new text box using the *Controls* group and enter the formula in the text box.

Reports often have different sections and certain computations can only be placed in certain sections. A grand total for the entire report must be placed in the *Report Footer*. A sub-totaling computation must be placed in the *Group Footer*. In this lesson, you will create two calculated fields: a text-based computation and a count of each client's trips.

1.   **If it is not already open, open the No Fault Travel database.**

2.   **Use the Report Wizard to create a report based on the following fields: *FirstName* and *LastName* in *TblClients*; and *DestinationID*, *DepartureDate*, *ReturnDate,* and *Cost* in *TblTrips*.**

3.   **When asked how to view the data, choose by *TblClients* and then click Next.**

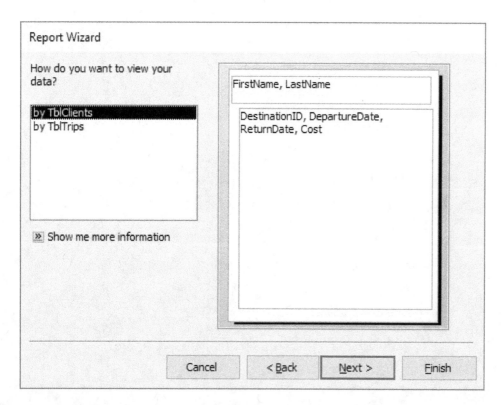

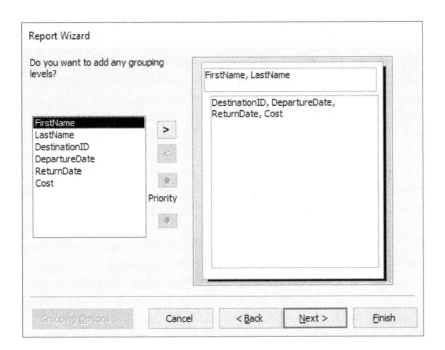

4. Do not add any additional grouping levels and click Next.

This report will already group by clients since you told Access that is how you wanted to view the data in the previous step.

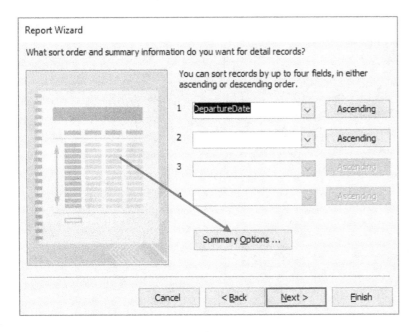

5. Choose to sort by *DepartureDate*. Click the *Summary Options...* button.

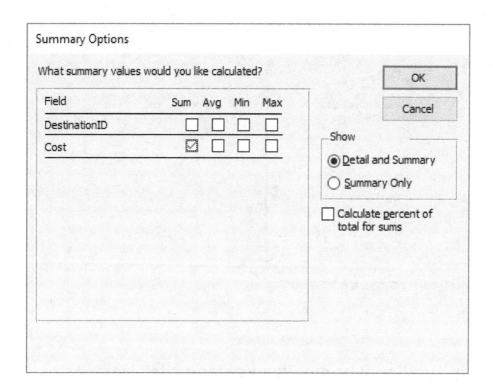

6. In the Summary Options dialog box, select *Sum* for *Cost*. Click OK and then click Next.

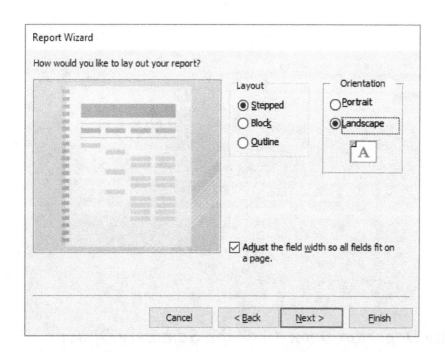

7. Choose *Stepped* Layout and *Landscape* Orientation. Click Next.

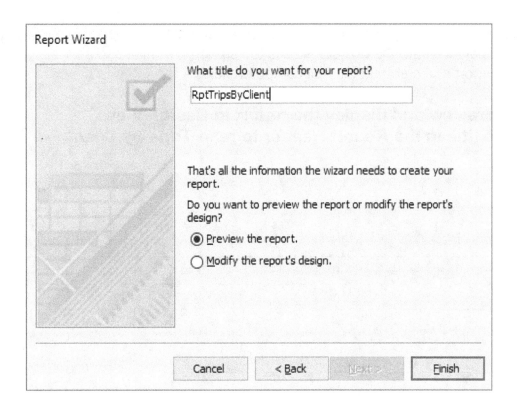

8. Title the report *RptTripsByClient* and click Finish.

A report preview should now be visible.

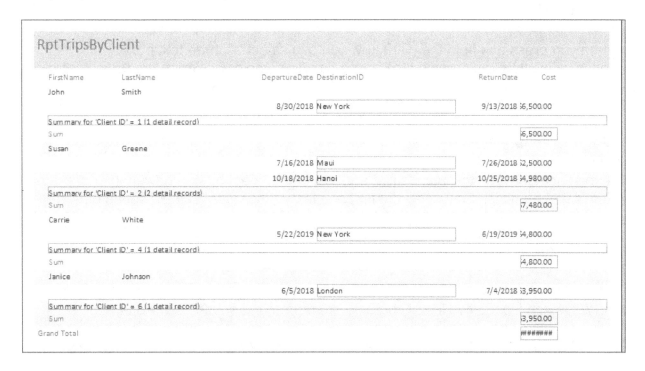

Some text boxes are not large enough to display the contained values. The hashtags (#) in the grand total field indicate the text box size is too small. We will make size adjustments to this report and create additional computed fields.

9. **Close the preview and display the report in Design View. Change the title in the *Report Header* to read *Trips by Client*.**

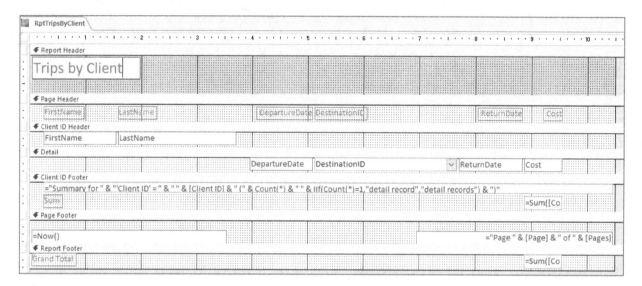

10. **Widen by about 0.5" the text boxes for the *Cost* and *Sum([Cost])* fields.**

When you press and hold the (Ctrl) key, you can select all three text boxes with the mouse. Size them by dragging the sizing handle to the right. Sizing the three controls (i.e., text boxes) at one time keeps their sizes uniform.

Concatenating text fields

This report displays the first and last names in separate text boxes. The amount of white space between the client's first and last names depends on how long or short the client's first name is. To display the first and last names with a single space between them, you will have to concatenate the two name fields into one field. In this portion of the lesson, you will create a text field that displays a client's name as the following example: Smith, Joe.

You will create a new text box and enter a formula in the text box that combines the two text fields and inserts two literal characters (comma and space) between them.

1. **In the *Page Header*, delete the *FirstName* and *LastName* labels.**

2. In the *Client ID Header*, delete the *FirstName* and *LastName* text boxes.

You will now create a text box which displays the first and last names together.

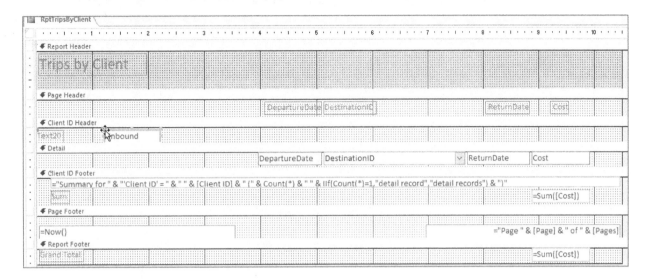

3. In the *Controls* group, click on the *Text Box* tool. Place a new text box in the *Client ID Header* section about 1" from the left edge of the page.

Be sure that you can see the label, which will be placed to the left of the new *Unbound* text box. The label needs to be visible to delete it. We will create a new label in *Page Header* as we did in the previous lesson.

4. Delete the label of the new text box. Then drag the left edge of the new text box to the left edge of the page. Adjust right edge of the text box to about the 2" mark on the horizontal ruler.

5. Copy one of the labels in the *Page Header*. Move it above the new text box and change the label to *Client Name*.

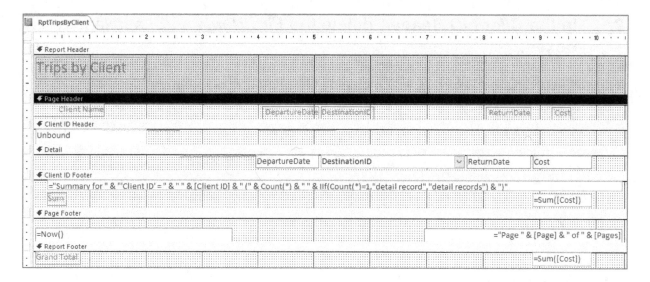

Resize the Page Header, if necessary. In the next step, you will enter a formula in the new text box to concatenate the first and last name fields.

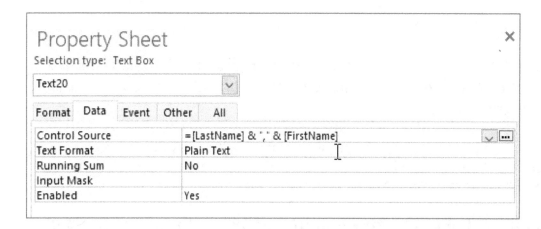

6.   **Display the Property Sheet of the new text box. For *Control Source* on the Data tab, type =[LastName]&", "&[FirstName].**

There is a space after the comma in the quotation marks, which are required for literal text. The ampersands (&) instruct Access to also include whatever follows in the text box.

7.   **Preview the report to ensure that the clients' names look similar in format to those in the following report.**

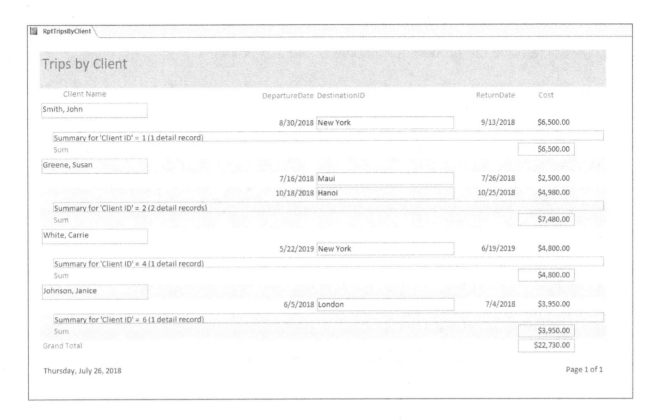

We will now make some additional formatting changes to improve the appearance of the report.

8. Return to Design View of this report.

9. In the ClientID Footer section select and then delete the very top control.

This control prints "Summary for ClientID…" and is not necessary for this report.

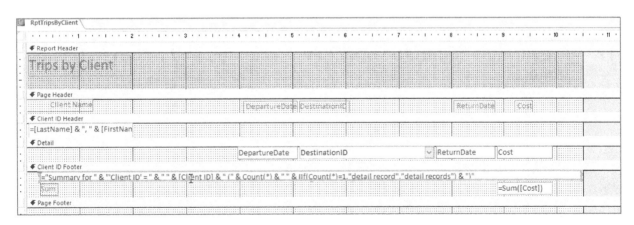

Now we will remove the borders from some of the text boxes.

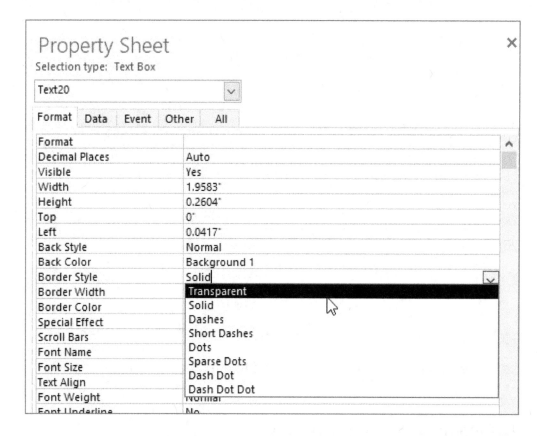

10. Select the textbox for the client's name and display the Property Sheet. In the Format tab, change the *Border Style* to *Transparent*.

11. Repeat Step 10 for the *DestinationID* and the two *Sum([Cost])* text boxes.

12. Preview the report to verify those changes and return to Design View.

Trips by Client

Client Name	DepartureDate	DestinationID	ReturnDate	Cost
Smith, John				
	8/30/2018	New York	9/13/2018	$6,500.00
Sum				$6,500.00
Greene, Susan				
	7/16/2018	Maui	7/26/2018	$2,500.00
	10/18/2018	Hanoi	10/25/2018	$4,980.00
Sum				$7,480.00
White, Carrie				
	5/22/2019	New York	6/19/2019	$4,800.00
Sum				$4,800.00
Johnson, Janice				
	6/5/2018	London	7/4/2018	$3,950.00
Sum				$3,950.00
Grand Total				$22,730.00

Friday, July 27, 2018   Page 1 of 1

You will now add a field to count the number of trips. This will be a summary computation. You included the concatenated name field in the *Detail* section because every record had this calculated field. Since you want to count the number of trips booked by each client, so you will place the summary computation in the *Client ID Footer*.

13. Return to Design View of this report.

14. Create a new text box and place it directly above the control that reads =Sum([Cost]) in the *Client ID Footer*.

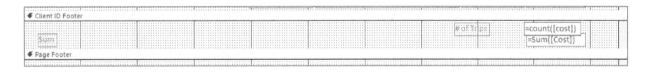

15. Change the new label to read *# of Trips*. In the new text box, type *=Count([Cost])*.

You can type the formula directly into the textbox or you can use the Property Sheet. The formula will count the number of times a cost appears in this section (which displays the trips booked by each client). This formula could have counted another field, but generally numeric fields work best in formulas.

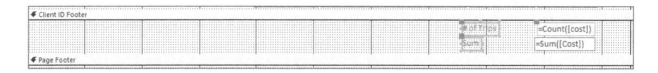

16. Move and align both labels and textboxes in the *Client ID Footer*.

Move the labels to the left of the return date field. You may want to experiment with the *Align* tool in the *Arrange* tab to align the textbox labels and controls.

17. On the Property Sheet Format tab for the *Count* textbox, change the *Border Style* to *Transparent*.

If you do not change the border style, the new text box will have a border.

18. Preview the report to verify you have entered the formula correctly.

If necessary to improve the report's appearance, return to Design View and make sizing or positioning adjustments.

Controlling Page Breaks

Currently, this report only creates a new page when the previous page is completely full. If the clients in this database scheduled more trips, it may be helpful to have each client's information start on a new page.

In this portion of the lesson you will have Access create a new page each time the *ClientID* changes. You can control page breaks in the format properties for the section you want to change. To create a new page with each client, you will add a page break to the *ClientID Header*.

1. **Return to the Design View of the report and click on the *Client ID Header* bar. Display the Property Sheet for this section.**

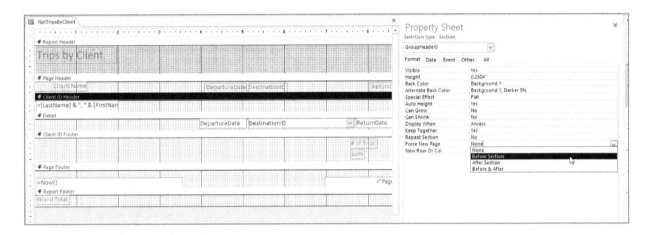

2. **Set the *Force New Page* property to *Before Section*.**

The *Force New Page* property inserts a page break before displaying a new client, so that each client begins on a new page. One client's trips may take several pages, but each client starts on a new page.

3. **Close the Property Sheet and save. Click the *View* tool on the ribbon and select *Print Preview*.**

Report View does not show page breaks, but *Print Preview* does. Now, each client's trips should appear on a new page. In the next steps, we will add page breaks after the main title and before the grand total.

4. **Close *Print Preview* and return to *Design View*.**

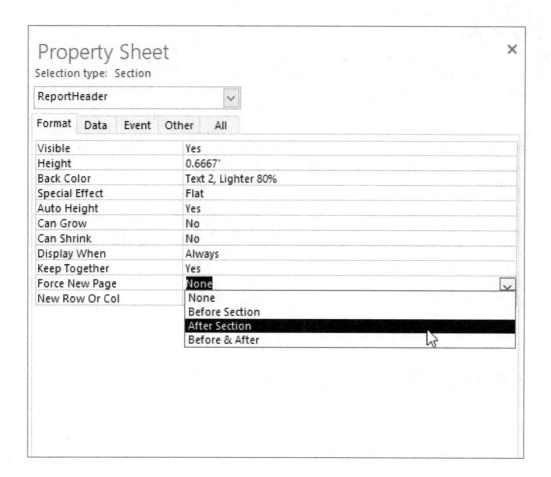

5. **Display the Property Sheet for the *Report Header*. Change the *Force New Page* property to *After Section*.**

6. **Display the Property Sheet for the *Report Footer*. Change the *Force New Page* property to *Before Section*.**

7. **Save and view in *Print Preview*.**

The report title and grand total should now appear on separate pages.

8. **Close *Print Preview* and the report.**

Lesson #8: Creating and Using Macros

In this lesson you will learn to:

Create Macros
Tie Macros to Events
Create Conditional Macros

Lesson #8: Creating and Using Macros

Macros allow you to automate repetitive tasks. You can create a macro to run a particular report, or even to open a certain form and find a specific record. In this lesson, you will create a macro to automatically set a trip's return date after a departure date is entered. This macro will set different trip lengths based on destination. Macros are very useful in forms.

Macros execute when they are triggered by an event. An event might be clicking a "Run Report" button. An event might be changing the value in a field.

Creating macros

Macros can be created by using the *Event tab* in the *Property Sheet* or the *Macro tool* on the ribbon's *Create tab*. Either way, you must link the macro to the control and to the event you want to trigger the macro.

You will now create a macro that runs the trip report and tie it to a button you will create in the clients form.

1.   **If not already open, open the No Fault Travel database. On the Create tab, click the *Macro* tool in the *Macros & Code* group.**

The Macro Builder should open. Unlike other Microsoft Office programs, you do not record macros to create them in Access.

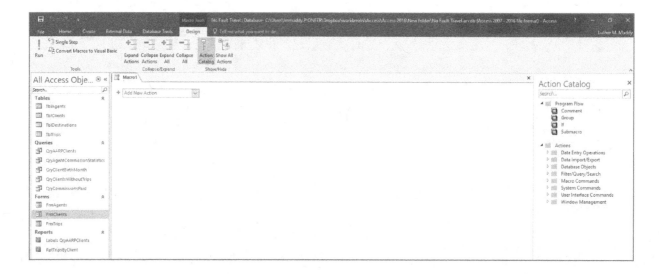

2.   **In the *Add New Action* dropdown list just below the Macro tab, click the dropdown arrow to open the list.**

3.   **From the list of commands, choose *OpenReport*.**

The *OpenReport* command will cause Access to open a report. In the next step, you will specify which report you want to open.

4.   Click the dropdown list arrow in the *Report Name* text box and choose *RptTripsByClients*.

The next step is to specify how you want to view the report: in Design View, Report View, Print Preview, or in print (on paper).

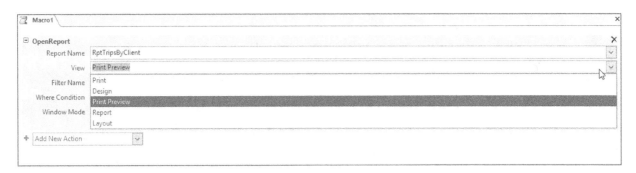

5. **Click the dropdown list arrow in the *View* text box and choose *Print Preview*.**

When you run this macro it will open the report in Print Preview mode.

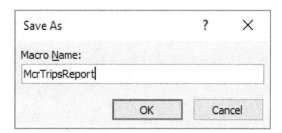

6. **Save this macro as *McrTripsReport* and close it.**

You may need to close both the macro and Macro Builder. The macro is now complete.

Linking an event to a macro

After creating the macro, the next step is to open the form that contains the control you want to link with the macro. You set the control's *Event Properties* to the specific event you want to trigger the macro. In this portion of the lesson you will create a button in the clients form and then link the report macro to the button. The macro will run when you click the button you are about to create.

1. **Open *FrmClients* in Design View.**

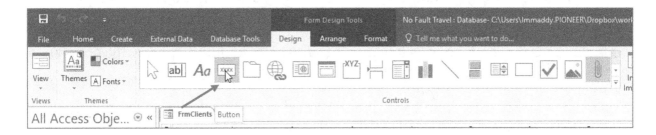

2. **In the Controls group on the Design tab, expand the Controls group and ensure the Use Control Wizards option is selected. Then, locate and click the Button tool.**

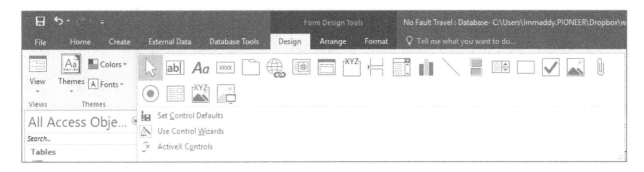

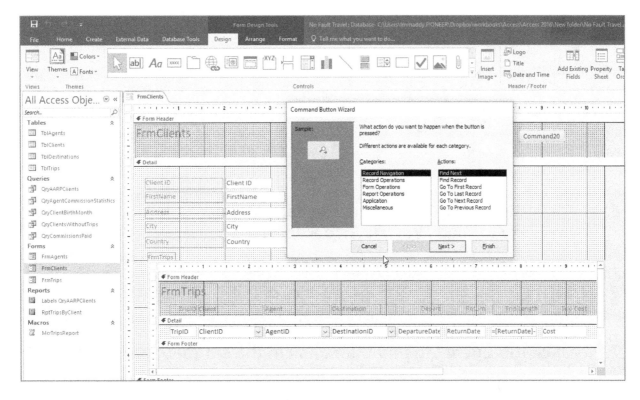

3. **Move the mouse pointer to an empty area in the Form Header section and click.**

You will now see the Command Button Wizard dialog box. The Command Button Wizard would help you build Visual Basic code to automate operations like opening forms and reports. This feature is often easier to use than creating macros. The advantage of creating macros is that macros are easier to modify for specific operations if you are not a Visual Basic programmer.

You could easily use the Command Button Wizard to cause this button to open the same report, but by creating and linking macros, you are also learning a little bit about events. Experimenting on your own with the Wizard will help you learn its power and how easy it is to use.

4.   Cancel the Command Button Wizard.

You will now see a button in this form. You will now change the text this button displays and link the macro you just created to this button.

5.   Select the button you just created. Right-click to open the shortcut menu and select *Properties*.

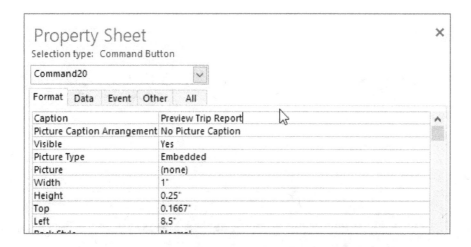

6.   Click the Format tab on the Property Sheet. Change the *Caption* property to read *Preview Trip Report.*

The button will display the *Caption* property text. Using the *On Click* property on the *Event* tab, you will attach the macro to the button, so that it runs when the button is clicked on.

7.   Click the *Event* tab and then click in the *On Click* property.

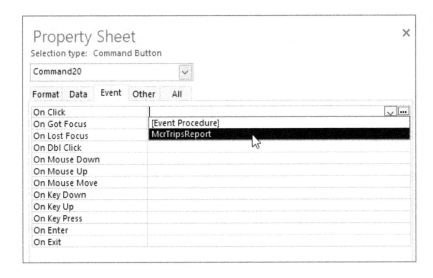

7. **Click the dropdown arrow in this row and select the macro**
***McrTripsReport*.**

When you click the dropdown arrow, all existing macros will be listed so that you can use the same macro in multiple places if you wish.

8. **Close the Property Sheet. Save the form and view in Form View. Click the *Preview Trip Report* button and verify that the macro works correctly.**

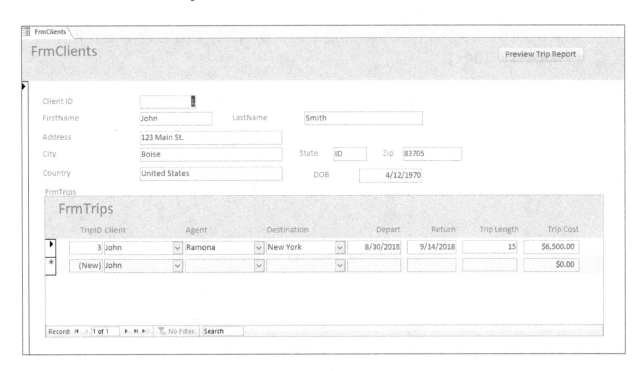

If needed, expand the Control button to display the entire text.

After clicking the button in the form you should be viewing the Trips report. If the macro does not work, go to the macros tab and open the macro. Make any needed corrections and try the process again.

10.   Close Print Preview.

You should now be back in the clients form.

11.   Close the clients form,

You will now create and link a macro that automatically sets the return date based in the departure date in the Trips Form.

The Set Value Action

The macro you are about to create will automatically set the return date once a departure date has been entered. We will assume that most trips are 10 days long. Our macro will use the *set value* action to set the return date equal to 10 days after the departure date.

The *set value* action allows you to enter expressions in equation arguments which will determine the value of the equation. In other words, the *set value* action will set the return date to a value equal to the *departure date + 10*.

1.   Place *FrmTrips* in Design View.

2.   Select the *DepartureDate* text box. Display the *Event* tab in the Property Sheet.

You will link the macro to the departure date field. After the user enters the departure date, the macro will set the return date in the return date field. In this exercise, you will create and tie the macro; in the previous exercise, the macro was created before you tied it to a control.

3.   Click in the *After Update* row and then click the build ⬚ button.

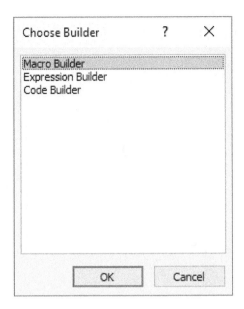

4.   In the *Choose Builder* dialog box, select Macro Builder and click
      OK.

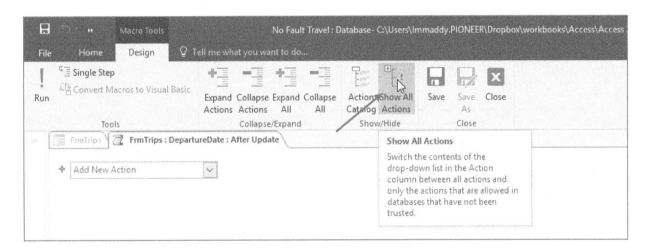

5.   In the Design tab, select the *Show All Actions* tool.

If this option is not selected, you will not be able to find the *SetValue* action that is
needed for the next step.

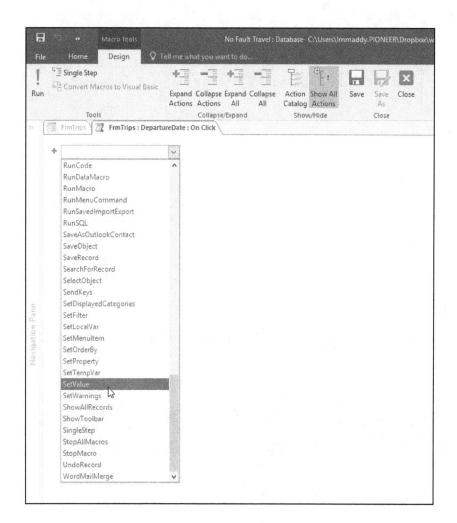

6.   Choose *SetValue* as the action from the dropdown menu.

The next step is to select which control you want to set the value of. You want this macro to set the return date.

7.   In the Item row, type *[ReturnDate]*.

Remember that Access always requires brackets when referencing field names.

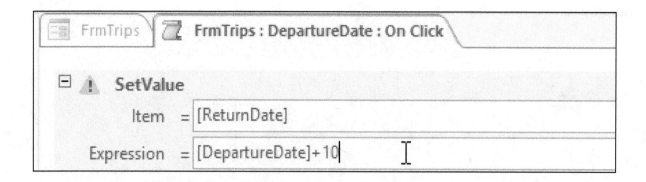

8. In the Expression row, type [DepartureDate]+10.

The expression is the value you want to appear in the return date field.

By default when the user enters a departure date, a return date 10 days later than the departure date appears in the return date field.

Using conditions in macros

The macro schedules all trips as 10 days in length, but the return date can be changed by the data entry person. While the majority of trips scheduled by the No Fault Travel company are 10 days, trips to Hanoi or Paris are typically 15 days long. With the present macro, the user always has to change the return date for trips to Hanoi or Paris.

A more useful macro would use a 10-day trip length, unless the destination was Hanoi or Paris -- in which case, the trip length would be set to 15 days. To accomplish this, you will have to add a condition to the macro to check the destination before setting the return date.

1. On the Design tab, click the *Action Catalog* tool.

The Action Catalog task pane should appear. The Action Catalog allows you to include comments for documentation or to add complexity, such as conditions, to your macros. In this portion of the lesson, you will add a condition which changes some return dates to 15 days after departure, depending on the destination. You will also add documentation to each macro step.

2. Under *Program Flow* in the Action Catalog pane, double click Comment.

A text area should appear where you can describe what this macro step does.

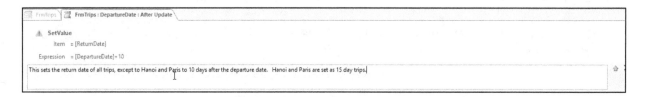

3. **In the comment area, type *This sets the return date of all trips, except to Hanoi and Paris to 10 days after the departure date. Hanoi and Paris are set as 15 day trips.***

The next step is to add the condition by selecting the *If* option under *Program Flow*. The condition will be dependent on the trip destination field, *DestinationID*.

In an earlier lesson, you created the *DestinationID* field as a lookup field on the trips table, which lists the destination (from the destination table). Although the destination dropdown list hides the destination ID, the *DestinationID* field actual stores the identification number for each destination. Therefore, the condition you will use to select Hanoi will be [DestinationId]=1 not [DestinationId]="Hanoi".

The table *TblDestinations* below shows the respective identification numbers for each destination. To prove to yourself that the *DestinationID* field in *TblTrips* and *FrmTrips* is a number, open *TblTrips* in Design View and notice that the *DestinationID* field (which is entered, modified and viewed in *FrmTrips*) has a number data type.

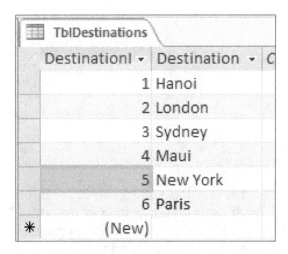

4. **Under *Program Flow* in the Action Catalog pane, double click *If*.**

You should now see that Access has added rows to enter the condition and the action to take if the condition is met.

5. In the *If* row, type *[DestinationID]=1 Or [DestinationID]=6.*

6. Click in the "Add New Action" box and select *SetValue*. Enter *[ReturnDate]* in the Item row and *[DepartureDate]+15* in the Expression row.

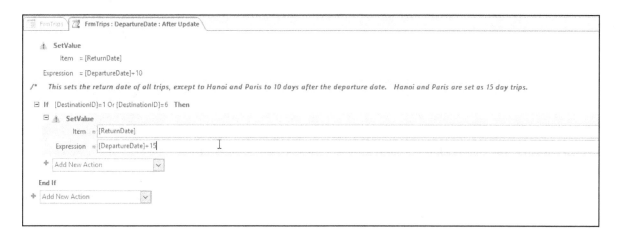

7. On the Design tab, click the *Save* tool to save this macro. Close the Action Catalog and macro after saving.

You are now ready to test this macro.

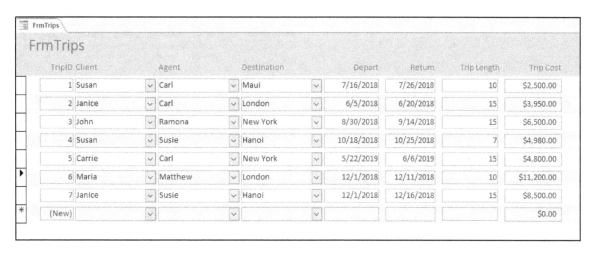

8. Save the trips form and display it in Form View. Add the two new trips shown above.

As soon as you enter the departure date for the two new trips, the return date field should auto populate as 10 to 15 days after departure, depending on the destination.

9. Close the trips form, *FrmTrips*.

Lesson #9: Parameter and Action Queries

In this lesson you will learn to:

> *Create and Use Action Queries*
> *Create and Use Parameter Queries*

Lesson #9: Parameter and Action Queries

Using Parameter Queries

Parameter queries allow you to change certain criteria based on parameters entered by the user to obtain specific information from the database. In a previous lesson, you created a query that computed each client's birth month based on the client's birthdate.

In this lesson, you will create a parameter query, which asks you to enter the numeric month for clients with birthdays falling in that month. Imagine creating mailing labels based on this query. As you open the mailing labels report, Access would instantly ask which birth month you wanted to print labels for. If you wanted labels for all clients with a May birthday, you would enter a 5 when prompted.

1. **If it is not already open, open the No Fault Travel database. View the query named *QryClientBirthMonth* in Design View.**

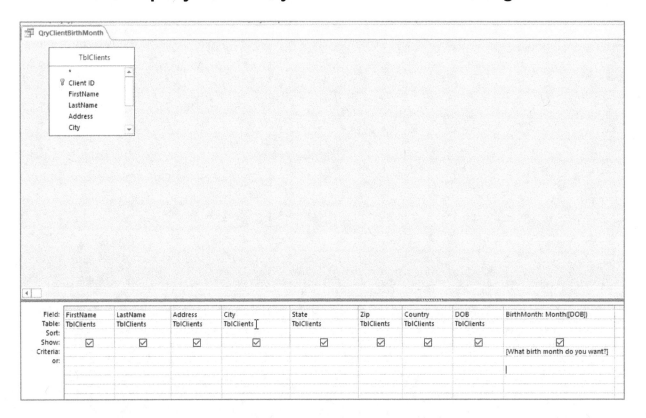

2. **In the criteria of the BirthMonth field type *[What birth month do you want?]*.**

This is the parameter. When you run the query, an *Enter Parameter Value* dialog box will appear and ask what birth month you want.

3. **Save and close this query.**

You will now use this query to create mailing labels by saving the existing label report under another file name and changing the query that the "new" label report is based on.

4.   In the navigation pane under *Reports*, double click on *LabelsQryAARPClients* and view in Design View.

5.   Click the File menu and choose the *Save As* option.

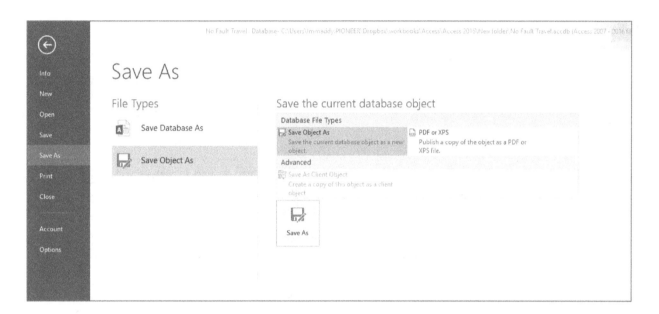

6.   Under *File Types*, choose *Save Object As*. Under *Save the current database object*, choose *Save Object As* and then click the *Save As* button.

Choosing *Save Object As* informs Access you are intending only to save the active object (i.e., the query) and not the entire database.

7.   In the *Save As* dialog box, name the new file *Labels Birthday Cards* and click OK.

8.   View *Labels Birthday Cards* in Design View. Without clicking anywhere in the labels, choose *Property Sheet* in the Tools group on the Design tab.

Be sure you are viewing the property sheet for entire report and not just a section or a field. If *Report* is not listed after *Selection type*, you can use the dropdown list to select it.

9.   On the Property Sheet pane, select the Data tab. Click the dropdown list arrow in the *Record Source* property.

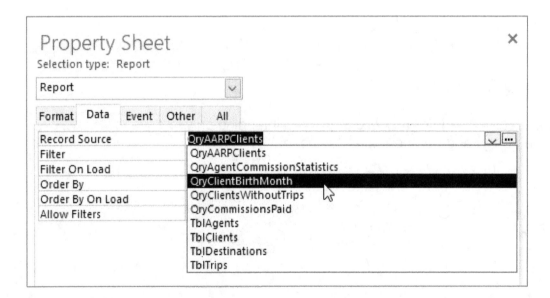

10. Change the *Record Source* to *QryClientBirthMonth* and then close the Properties dialog box.

11. Save and close the report.

Now, you will open the labels tied to the birth month query.

12.   In the navigation pane under *Reports*, double click the *Labels Birthday Cards* report.

Because the label report is based on the parameter query, Access now asks you to specify which birth month you want.

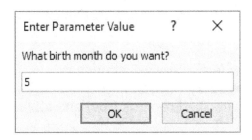

13.   In the *Enter Parameter Value* dialog box, type *5* and then click OK.

You should now be viewing labels for clients with a May birthday.

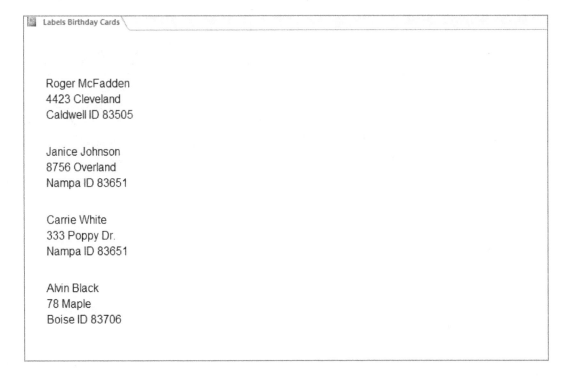

14.   Close the label report.

15.   Run the label report again, and enter *12* as the birth month.

Notice there are different labels.

16.   Close the resulting label report.

Working with action queries

All the queries you have used in this class so far are variations of a *Select* query. *Select* queries allow you to view data and even compute values based on query fields. *Select* queries do not change the data in the tables. On the other hand, *action* queries can add, change, or delete the data in tables.

Access provides several types of *action* queries. The *update* query will change or update data, based on the criteria you enter. The *delete* query will delete records that meet the criteria you specify. *Make table* queries copy specified records from one table to a new table.

Creating an update query

In this portion of the lesson, you will create an update query that increases by 1% the commission rate of all agents who have scheduled trips to Maui.

1.   Create a new query in Design View based on *TblAgents, TblTrips* and *TblDestinations.*

2.   Add the *CommissionRate* field from *TblAgents* and *Destination* from *TblDestinations.*

You added the destinations table and are using the destination field (not destination ID) from that table so you can use "Maui" in the criteria and not the identification number for "Maui" as you did when making macros.

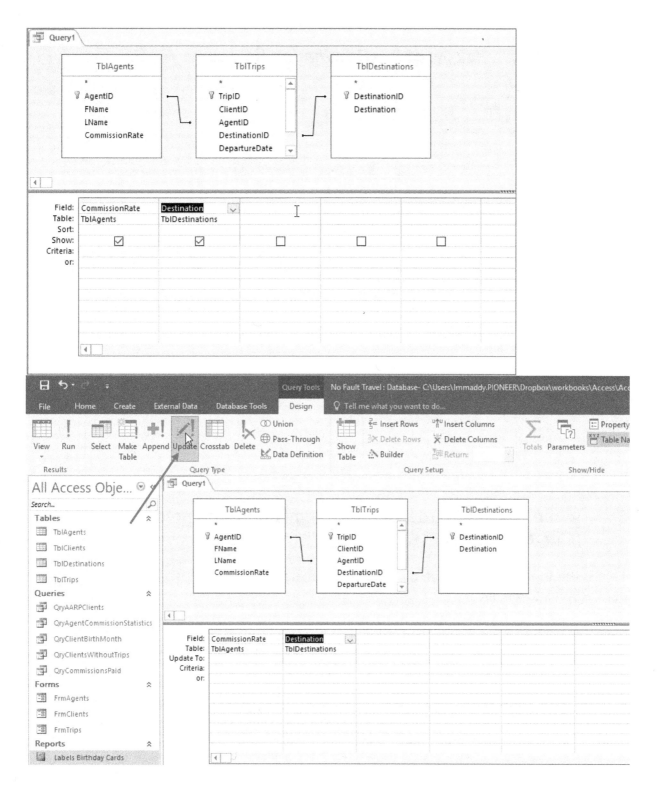

## 3.	From the *Query Type* group in the Design tab, choose *Update* query.

This changes the query type to *update*. You should notice a new row in query design labeled *Update To*.

4. In the *Criteria* row of the *Destination* field, type *Maui*.

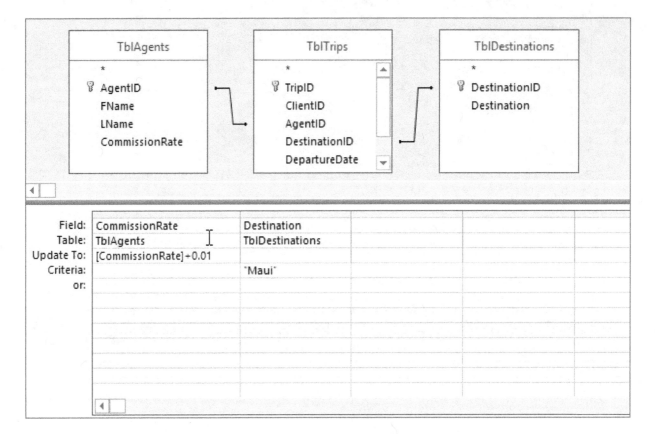

5. In the *Update To* row in the *CommissionRate* field, type **[CommissionRate]+.01**.

This is the formula to increase by 1% the commission rates of those agents who have booked trips to Maui.

Note: To run an action query from Design View, you must use the *! Run* tool in the *Results* group on the *Design* ribbon. The *View* tool in the *Results* group works great for running *select* queries but not *action* queries.

6. Save this query as *QryIncreaseCommissions* and close it.

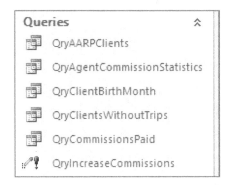

Notice that the action query you just saved has a different icon in the navigation pane object list than the select queries on the list. **Be extremely cautious when you run action queries.** You might consider not saving them at all.

Every time you run the update query you just created, the commission rates of agents with trips to Maui will be increased. Running the query multiple times would result in extremely high commissions for the lucky agents.

You will run the query once in this course – just to see how an action query works. Since this is fictitious data, you may run it multiple times just for fun.

7.   In the list of queries, open *QryIncreaseCommissions.*

8.   Answer Yes when asked if you want to continue.

This is a warning message telling you to use caution when running Action queries.

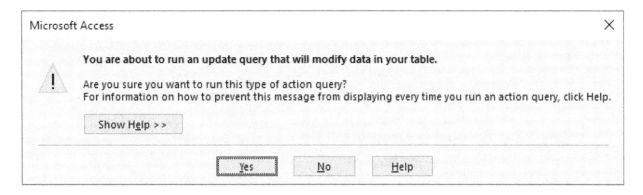

Access now tells you how many records this query will update. Your number may be different if you have modified or entered additional fictitious data.

9.   Answer Yes when asked if you want to update the rows.

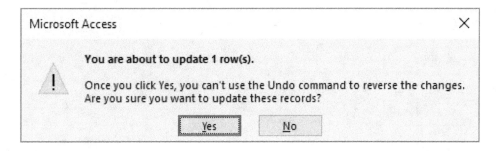

After clicking yes here, you will not see any confirmation that the query has run. To verify that the query has modified the commission rates in the agents table, you can examine the records in that table.

10. Open *TblAgents* in Datasheet View.

If you compare the before and after agents table, you will see that Carl Lee has received an increase in his commission rate because he booked a trip to Maui.

Before:

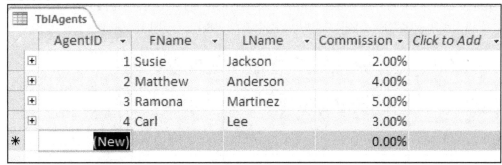

After:

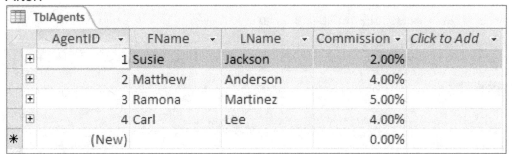

11. Close the table.

Index

Other books that may interest you

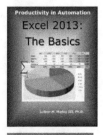
Excel: The Basics (2016, 2013 or 2010)
In "learning by doing" you will gain a good grasp of the basics of Excel. You'll learn to create formulas, format and print worksheets, copy and move cell data, and generate attractive charts and graphs from your Excel data.

Retail price: $10.95

Access: The Basics (2016, 2013)
In this course Access users will learn to: Understand Basic Database Design Techniques Create, Modify and Use Tables Create, Modify and Use Forms Create, Modify and Use Reports and Mailing Labels Create Database Relationships Enter, Edit, and Find Records Create, Edit and Use Queries Use Field Properties and Validation Rules Add Drop-down Lists to Forms
Retail price: $12.95

Excel: Database and Statistical Features (2016, 2013 or 2010)
In "learning by doing" you will gain a good grasp of the Excel database features. You'll learn to create and use Pivot Tables and Charts. You'll also learn about database functions like DSum() and DAverage(). You'll also learn about filtering and subtotaling Excel data. Finally, you'll learn about performing statistical analysis using the Analysis Toolpak.

Retail price: $9.95

Word: The Basics (2016, 2013 or 2010)
In "learning by doing" you will learn the basics of MS Word. You'll also be introduced to performing tasks the most efficient way possible to increase your productivity. This workbook covers document creation and editing. You'll learn to copy and move and enhance text. You'll also learn about page a paragraph formatting, setting tabs, creating tables and more.

2013: Retail price: $9.95   2010: Retail price: $8.95

Word: Enhancing Documents (2013 or 2010)
In "learning by doing" you will learn the some of the desktop publishing features of Word. You'll learn to place text in columns, use Autoshapes, enhance mailing labels, and use and create styles. You'll also learn to add hyperlinks to your documents, how to use pre-defined templates, and much more.

2013: Retail price: $9.95   2010: Retail price: $8.95

PowerPoint: The Basics (2016, 2013 or 2010)
In this "learning by doing" course you will learn to: Create and run presentations, Apply and modify design themes, Insert clipart, audio, and video clips, Apply and use slide transitions, Print audience handouts and speaker notes and much more

Retail price: $9.95

Order wherever books are sold. Ordering in quantity?
Save up to 20% by ordering on our website: www.Pro-aut.com